Tools for Transforma

Tools for Transformation
Making Worship Work

PETER CRAIG-WILD

DARTON·LONGMAN+TODD

First published in 2002 by
Darton, Longman and Todd Ltd
1 Spencer Court
140–142 Wandsworth High Street
London SW18 4JJ

ISBN 0–232–52449–1

A catalogue record for this book is available from the British Library.

Designed by Sandie Boccacci
Phototypeset in 9.75/13pt Utopia
by Intype London Limited
Printed and bound in Great Britain by
Page Bros, Norwich, Norfolk

This book is dedicated to

ROSE SURR

1948–2001

A wonderful Christian and a dear friend whose relatively unexpected death meant that I was never able to say thank you for the words of encouragement she gave, the fun we shared, the sanctuary she offered and for the love and hospitality her family had shown us over many years. I hope this dedication goes some way now to making up for my lack of expressions of gratitude while she was still with us here on earth.

May she rest in peace and rise in glory!

I would like to thank my wife Dhoe for her encouragement and support, and for teaching me English again, Helen Butler who sensitively commented on the text and the ideas in it, John Leach whose persistence persuaded me to put pen to paper, and Michelle and John for their proofreading. Thank you all the musicians of Wellspring who have so often helped me turn half-worked-out ideas into reality. I would also like to thank the staff of DLT, and especially my editors, Katie and Kathy, who at times seemed to have more confidence in me than I ever had in myself.

And to my Mum and Dad – simply thank you!

Contents

Foreword ix

Introduction   Hopes and Frustrations   1

Chapter 1   Word, Word, Word!   4

Chapter 2   Worship in Four Dimensions   21

Chapter 3   Transforming Worship   30

Chapter 4   Living Worship   53

Chapter 5   Parabolic Worship   69

Chapter 6   Symbolic Worship   80

Chapter 7   Engaging Worship   100

Chapter 8   Creating Worship   122

Conclusion   Freeing Worship   144

Notes   147

Foreword

So, what was the service like? Was it a good service? Simple questions to ask, but how difficult to answer. Who is to say? Did the congregation think it was good, or at least some of them? How did the person leading feel about it? Uplifting, boring, routine, too long, didn't like the sermon/prayers/new hymns/ whatever – or was it just OK? What a variety of responses we are likely to get. What standard – whose standard – do we apply? And how would an expert assess it? What would a liturgist say?

Peter Craig-Wild is a liturgist as well as a gifted parish priest. Liturgists, it is rumoured, are given to the Church so that in times when we are spared persecution, we may still know suffering. (A bishop said that to me, not another layperson). Most Christians are wary of those who are knowledgeable about worship. They fear that the simple is being made complicated. All specialities can seem like a conspiracy against the laity. But when an enthusiast for worship shares his understanding and insight, we are shaken out of our wariness (and weariness).

It is not enough to be knowledgeable. Connoisseurs of worship are to be avoided. Marks out of ten for technical merit and artistic expression show we are missing the point. Stars may be a good guide for restaurants, but not for church services. Worship should involve us and engage us; we are not to be observers only and worship is not a spectator sport. Its purpose is to bring us into encounter with our God.

Yet often the worship we experience leaves us dissatisfied, and we are not sure why. Somehow it has not gathered us in, engaged our attention and our hearts, and that is not always or entirely our fault. We are no longer satisfied just by using familiar words. Those who lead may often sense that something more is required, but the gift of leading worship well is rare, and certainly rarer than those who lead seem to believe.

Peter has produced a book to help both the leaders and the led. He races along with verve, throwing out ideas, comments and asides, reminding us of things we have forgotten, showing us what we ought to have known, and often giving us insights which are real disclosure moments, 'Yes, that's right!' we want to say.

Peter is a gifted leader of worship, but a practical one. 'Does it work?' is the touchstone. Does it bring us closer to God? If it doesn't work, at that level, it is bad liturgy.

The Church of England has busied itself with alternative official texts for worship since 1965 – cautious at first, but moving on to the ASB in 1980, and more recently *Common Worship*. But new words (and plenty of them) are not the whole answer. 'Words, words, words, I'm so sick of words . . .'. sings Eliza in *My Fair Lady*. 'If you're in love, *show* me. . .' Peter mirrors that in respect of our worship, showing us what else we need to engage us wholly and lift us to the Gate of Heaven.

This is exciting stuff – it is encouraging, and I am delighted to commend it.

John W. Bullimore
MEMBER OF GENERAL SYNOD AND READER

Hopes and Frustrations

It was a sunny day at the end of June. The sound of cathedral bells floated over the Ripon rooftops announcing that a new army of clergy would be on its way to tackle and solve the problems of the Church and the world. I was one of them.

We had reason to be hopeful. Soon the Church of England was about to experience the most radical liturgical revolution since 1662. It was 1980, the year in which the Alternative Service Book, the new collection of modern-language services, would be introduced. The excitement built up as we approached 1 November, the first day on which we would be allowed to use the new rites. There were many, and I was one, who thought that the introduction of this new modern-language prayer book would signal a filling, instead of an emptying, of church pews. We really were convinced that if we revised the words of the liturgy it would inevitably lead to the renewal of the Church in England.

Frustrated hope

Twenty years on, as those of us in the Church of England face another round of liturgical revision, there are few who hold those high expectations about *Common Worship*. Those with an interest in liturgy are excited because it presents new creative possibilities, but most seem to approach *Common Worship* with a grudging acceptance rather than unfettered excitement.

I have no doubt that change was needed in 1980. The language of worship was woefully out of touch with the language of everyday people and almost every English-speaking Church had revised, or was in the process of revising, its liturgy into modern English. Naturally there were those who strongly protested, having a deep affection for the Book of Common Prayer, but their cries were greater than their numbers. Those same voices can still be heard, and some congregations have continued to thrive while remaining faithful to the 'Thees and Thous' of BCP, but they remain a minority. A few actually thrive, but there are dangers in being a market leader for a dying product.

So the liturgical revisions of the past twenty or thirty years have gone ahead. The Churches have been swimming with the current on the need for linguistic change. New and modern-language services have been produced, but many conduct them as they have always done, consequently worship has changed little. Clergy the length and breadth of England embraced the new texts, perhaps not realising that we need not primarily a change of words but a change in our approach to worship.

I have spoken with some of those responsible for the introduction of the ASB in 1980, and it was clearly their intention that there should be some accompanying liturgical formation, but in practice this has been hard to achieve. One problem is that many ministers consider themselves experts at preparing and leading worship, and consequently develop an inbuilt resistance to liturgical training. Sometimes the reverse is true – ministers may think they *ought* to be experts in worship, know they aren't, and feel too embarrassed to talk about it. Whatever the reason, little formation has happened and the opportunity to look at how we 'do' worship, rather than just what we 'say' in worship, has passed us by.

A failing Church

For some time now the Western Church has been facing a crisis of confidence that has had a deep impact on its life and worship. To its credit it has recognised the problem, but so far seems to have failed to find any effective solution. Finances and worshippers are in increasingly short supply; morale among clergy and committed lay people seems to be at an all-time low; and confidence seems to be as rare as a blue diamond. The press constantly assaults the Churches with stories about child abuse, falling numbers of baptisms, marriages and confirmations, moral lapses and over-spending bishops. There is no respite. At the same time worship is competing with the attractions of the electronic, consumer society: 'Who wants to read the lesson at Evensong?' against *Who Wants to Be a Millionaire?* and Bible study against *Match of the Day.*

So what has gone wrong?

There is no one answer to such a complex question but one possibility is that the Church has failed to take account of the cultural revolution happening around us. The Church is speaking less and less in the language of our changing world and is consequently less and less able to communicate the Gospel. This is equally true of the language of worship. What the revisers of the 1980s could not have known was how our culture, not just our language, would change. Further down the line we are becoming aware that a renewal of our approach to worship is needed, not just a revision of the text. The question I am concerned with is 'How can we make worship work today?'

Trying to understand what is happening, and has happened over the past two decades, has led me to write this book. There was an innocence about my assumptions in 1980. During my diaconal year I was shocked by what I thought was the cynicism of one of the senior clergy in my deanery. He asked, 'Don't you think it is naïve to believe that by changing the words people say in the services we will change the love in their hearts for God?' In retrospect that was a poignant question. Renewed-language services have clearly failed to produce renewed congregations. Consciously or unconsciously, ministers across the world have learned that you do not change the hearts of the worshippers just by changing the words of worship. The tools needed to meet the challenge of renewing our worship are very different from the ones employed to enable liturgical revision, and it is the tension between them that I want to wrestle with here.

Chapter 1

Word, Word, Word!

It was Saturday evening at a worship festival in Jersey. We had used a symbolic form of confession, a style that was new to everyone. Each person was given a small piece of red wool. After a period of reflection using music, images and silence we sang 'Lord, have mercy; Christ, have mercy; Lord, have mercy'. We tied the pieces of wool, representing our sins, onto long pieces of red rope and passed them over our heads to the next row. Eventually the song finished. In silence the ropes were brought forward and dumped on a large, rough, freestanding cross. The silence continued for some time before the absolution was pronounced. The effect was dramatic.

At the end of the evening the leader of a local independent charismatic church asked if he could borrow the cross and the ropes for his church's worship the following day, promising to return it on Monday. On Monday he came back full of excitement at the impact the cross and ropes had made on his congregation the previous day. One person in particular had approached him at the end of the service and said, 'Mike, you have taught about the cross many times and I must admit it, I haven't really got it. But finally I can see it!' Mike added that he needed to think more about how he could use symbol in worship.

We are obsessed with words. This is not surprising considering that the roots of the modern Western Church are firmly planted in the theological melting-pot of the fifteenth and sixteenth centuries. The Reformation and the Enlightenment have been the soil in which the Churches have been rooted and the air that they have breathed. They were word-based times and have generated a word-based Church with word-obsessed worship.

This chapter aims to point to the ways in which a modern, rationalistic worldview has emerged out of the cultural and philosophical soup of the past five centuries. In these few pages I can only offer a brief sketch, really no more than a cartoon. The process is far more complex than can be presented here but I hope to make the point that we are a word/mind-obsessed people.[1]

A new technology and a new culture

The sleepiness of the Middle Ages was stirred by an invention that would change the world for ever. It was the printing press. When Johann Gutenberg printed the German Bible in 1455 he could not have realised the impact he would have on the culture and development of the western world. The printing press was the Internet of its day, transforming communication and making knowledge, including theological and biblical scholarship, much more widely available. It also led to the development of a word-based culture that had a profound impact on the way people thought, and the way the Church engaged with both theology and worship.

Before 1455 liturgical texts could only be reproduced by hand. This required lengthy, painstaking effort on the part of dedicated and often artistic monks who made handwritten copies of manu-scripts, taking years in the process. Liturgical uniformity was impossible to enforce. Texts could not be produced quickly enough or at an affordable price to make it practical. Con-sequently, a rite might be authorised at the centre but there was no way its use could be imposed on the rest of the Church, so local rites proliferated, some of greater value than others, and few of which now remain.

It was the invention of the printing press that put an end to this freedom. Suddenly, authorised texts could be produced relatively cheaply and quickly. It is ironic that this invention, which in so many ways led to the freeing of minds, was also the invention that enabled the imposition of liturgical correctness, whether it was from Rome, Geneva or Canterbury. Without the invention of the printing press the concept of 'common prayer' simply would not have been possible and the Book of Common Prayer would have remained as much a figment of the imagination as Leonardo da Vinci's helicopter.[2]

The printing press allowed liturgical texts to become more widely available. It was possible to insist that the same words were used in every church on the same day – and because such power was possible, it was used. Although Henry VIII had severed the connection with Rome in 1534 it was his son, Edward VI, who used this power to impose the first English communion service in 1549. Over the next decade the pendulum would swing fully both ways. An even more Protestant prayer book followed in 1552 only to be replaced by a return to the Latin Mass, when Catholic Queen Mary succeeded her brother. Finally, when Elizabeth followed Mary, it settled somewhere in the middle and the *via media* was established as the norm of Anglicanism. However, over these turbulent ten years the printed word had enabled the imposition of liturgical uniformity, at least in the words that were used – and at that time words were all-important.

It didn't stop there. Soon the printing presses were hot with rubrics[3] telling the priests and people not only what they should *say* but also what they should and should not *do* in the Mass. The Act of Uniformity of 1559 marked the zenith of liturgical control-freakery. Priests were also told what must be worn and what posture should be adopted. It was as if worship had been reduced to rubric, and word became the determining element of worship.

The invention of the printing press had changed the ecclesiastical face of Western Europe and unleashed the power of the word.

The Reformation wrestling match

Although the printing press created the circumstances in which ecclesiastical uniformity could be imposed, the new technology also created an environment in which the protestors could make their mark. To a large extent the printing press made the Reformation possible and, as the free thinking mindset of the

Renaissance was applied to the monolith of the medieval Church, the new critique that would become the Reformation gathered pace. The result was the greatest upheaval that the Church has faced in its 2000-year history.

While the Churches imposed their own liturgical uniformity of word and rubric, we need to remember that these words were carefully chosen. Liturgical texts were being formulated against the background of a theological war in which words were the weapons. As Protestant and Catholic theologians wrestled verbally (and sometimes literally) over the meaning of the sacraments and salvation, the new liturgies of the emerging Protestant Churches reflected their changing beliefs. One of the major theological battlegrounds of the Reformation was the Eucharist, and the emerging texts were weapons in the war. The Protestant communion services were liturgical critiques of the Catholic theology of the Eucharist.

The Catholics counter-attacked at the Council of Trent in 1545. The new Tridentine Mass was not just an order of service but a powerful argument for the Catholic theology of the Eucharist. As James White has pointed out,[4] the Tridentine Mass is thoroughly a product of the Reformation and bears all the same cultural and philosophical marks as the 1559 Book of Common Prayer. Catherine Bell argues that although ceremony, ritual and symbol remained during the Reformation period the emphasis changed. Commenting on the Tridentine Mass she writes, 'The emphasis was not so much on what was done as on what was *said* – the words that made this miracle [of transubstantiation] occur.'[5] The effects of this were complex. While the balance of power moved from action to word, the new rubrics stifled local creativity and the emergence of local rites attuned to the local subcultures disappeared.

There is nothing better than a good fight to ensure a sharp sword and the Reformation sharpened the theological tools of all the protagonists. All parties demanded greater and greater theological precision to make their points ever more subtly. Words were at a premium. In the dialectical context of the age ambiguity was the sworn enemy of the theologian. Truth, precision, doctrine and word were not only at the top of the agenda, they were virtually the only items on it.

The Reformation was, if anything, the era of the Scriptures. Printing made Bibles widely available for the first time, and translations into the vernacular followed swiftly, making them more accessible to the Church at large. For the Reformers the Scriptures were the sole source of authority in the Church, and their identity was forged in the exposition of the Bible. The further education of the clergy was both inevitable and imperative as so much more was expected of them. Preaching and teaching became an integral part of priest-craft for both Protestant and Catholic alike, and all the major Protestant Churches aimed to make a university degree a necessary qualification for ordination. Though none achieved this there was considerable improvement in the education of the clergy. In 1573 the Bishop of Lincoln ordained 25 priests, 8 of whom had degrees. In 1583 he ordained 32, of whom 22 had degrees. Just two years later there were 399 graduate clergy in the Lincoln Diocese; in 1603 there were 648.[6]

Through these figures we can see the increasing intellectualisation of the clergy, which went hand in hand with the increasing significance of the role of the sermon in worship. Stricter Protestant churches insisted on two sermons each Sunday, though in reality this was not widespread. In the latter half of the sixteenth century some churches acquired a new piece of furniture. This was the hourglass by the pulpit. One hour was thought to be the maximum concentration span for a sermon. Consequently hourglasses and hour-long sermons became commonplace in English parish churches during Elizabethan times. Most churches demanded an hour-long sermon, and the other elements of the liturgy were squeezed out to ensure that the minister and congregation got home in time for lunch! The ministry of the word took over worship and we are still living with the consequences of this today.

The Reformation not only changed the shape of the institutional Church for ever, but it also transformed the expectations and presuppositions of the way it *did* liturgy. Suddenly liturgy became the main arena for a theological wrestling match that would last four hundred rounds, each lasting a year. Liturgy now became prescriptive of theology. Up to the beginning of the Reformation there were so many local rites that it would be impossible to use a eucharistic liturgy as the basis for determining eucharistic theology without reconciling a mass of contradictions. But now, the imposed uniform texts became the key weapons in the argument. The tendency for theology to dominate our liturgies is still prevalent today. The outcome of the Reformation debate was that theologians began to dominate worship.

From Reformation to Enlightenment

To some extent Protestantism began as a reaction to the quasi-magical spirituality and theology of medieval Catholicism, but it did not stay like that for long. It quickly developed its own theological and philosophical momentum. For Protestants the sacraments became more and more a pious memory exercise[7] as the focus moved from what God did/does in the sacraments to what individuals do. Reformation eucharistic theology gradually moved from the mystical approach of Catholicism, through Luther and Calvin, to the humanistic approach of Zwingli. The eucharistic action was reduced from a thing of great solemnity in the Mass to the simple repetition of the narrative of institution followed by the giving of the bread and wine.

I remember, as a first-year undergraduate, sitting in a lecture on the 'History of Christian thought'. I was totally new to both the department and subject of theology and had very recently made the huge academic leap from the chemistry department to reading philosophy and theology. Understandably I was slightly nervous, as I was a real fish out of water. It was halfway through the first term, and as I had missed the first half of the lecture course I had no idea what the lecturer was going on about. I was lost in a daze of words that had little meaning and was all too easily distracted by poetic thoughts about the autumn sun that warmed the world beyond the lecture room. In fact, in my head I was composing quite a romantic poem. Suddenly the dreaming was destroyed.

'And what was the principal mark of the Reformation?' It took a while for me to realise that the professor and head of department was actually addressing me. He repeated the question, which was helpful in one sense because I hadn't been listening the first time but unhelpful in another because I still had no idea what the answer was. I decided to guess with confidence – this is a strategy I have adopted frequently in my life and has served me well. 'The Bible,' I answered. From the look on his face I could see that it wasn't going to serve me well this time. 'Individualism!' he bellowed back, 'Individualism!' I have forgotten a great deal about the Reformation since then but I have never forgotten that. So I dedicate this short point to the Rt Revd and Prof. John Tinsley, formerly Bishop of Bristol, and Professor of Theology at Leeds University.

It had been a mark not only of the medieval Church but also of the medieval world that the individual didn't really count, with the exception of a titled few. The Reformation turned this on its head. The individual believer, rather than the Church, became the focus of the work of salvation; the individual believer had to declare his or her faith; the individual believer was justified by faith. The move from a church to an individual focus was a significant shift, which later gave the Protestant Churches the theological and ethical foundation on which to crusade for the abolition of slavery, the attack on poverty, and the growth of the trade union movement. Every individual counts.

This gradual change of emphasis from Church to individual brought its own set of philosophical problems. If the individual is so important, what is it that differentiates one individual from another? The answer to this question was one of the products of the thinking of the next philosophical wave.

The Enlightenment

The humanising tendency of the Reformation (WE remember – WE act) flowed naturally into the period of thought often called the Enlightenment. This period provided the philosophical and cultural foundation for the western world from the middle of the seventeenth century.

The Enlightenment is a term used to cover the period from around 1650 until about 1800. It is the crucible of the modern world. It was the period when reason became almost the sole criterion of judgement. Philosophers believed that there was a rational principle behind the universe and therefore the universe could be fully understood by applying reason to any problem. As the Reformation buzzwords were *word, truth* and *doctrine* so the Enlightenment buzzwords were *mind, knowledge* and *reason*.

The fires of the Reformation had run out of fuel and the thinkers of the day needed something new on which to exercise those now well-developed tools of precise thinking and philosophical word craft. They started to ask questions such as, 'How do we know?' 'How do we know something is the truth?' 'How do we know we even exist?' People were beginning to question whether even God existed.

René Descartes (1596–1650) was exercised by just that question. He longed to provide an answer to those who needed proof that God existed. He was irritated by the question, 'How do I know that God exists?' But he was frustrated even more by the fact that he couldn't prove there was an 'I' to do the knowing in the first place. At the time he was working as a tutor to Queen Christina of Sweden, so he sat for months on end in the oven in her kitchen to think about it all. Eventually his 'Eureka' moment came. '*Cogito, ergo sum!*' 'I think, therefore I am.' If 'I' am thinking there *must* be an 'I' to do it![8]

It is often suggested that this is the defining moment in modern western philosophy. The impact of the *Cogito* has been felt down the centuries. Its logical coherence, or lack of it, is neither here nor there. Its importance does not depend on its truth, but in the influence it has had on the development of our culture. Descartes' *Cogito* established the supremacy of thinking, of the mind as the centre of the human reality. Descartes, and those who followed him, awarded superiority to mental activity, claiming that the purest form of human activity was activity of the mind. Consequently, the ultimate relationship, which is our relationship with God, became supremely, even exclusively, a relationship involving the mind rather than the heart. Passion and love, intimacy and imagination, were banished to the sidelines.

Suspicion of externals

This fitted in comfortably with the Protestant suspicion of such things as symbol, ritual, images, elaborate architecture, indeed anything that might be labelled 'external' in worship. It was the mind that differentiated humans from the rest of creation and their minds that differentiated one individual from another. Worship would therefore appeal to the mind and true worship would be pure mental activity. Sacraments became a human act of remembering; prayer became a human act of concentration; theology became a human act of understanding. Anything that might distract the mind from its essential focusing on God was removed from worship and the worship space. One of the features of worship since the Enlightenment era has been its increasing minimalisation, even in mainstream churches.

I worked for four years at St David's Church in Beeston, Leeds, a 1960s' construction even though it was consecrated in 1971. Its architect, Mr Geoffrey Davy, wanted simplicity with no visual distractions. The interior is plain brick and the stained-glass windows are designed so that they cannot be seen by most of the worshipping congregation. There was not even a cross on the vast 24–foot high east wall, making St David's a good example of the style of liturgical architecture that results in worship being reduced to a mental activity.

The combined effects of the Reformation and the Enlightenment on worship have been immense. They have asserted, and much thinking about worship now assumes, the superiority of:

- mind over body;
- conscious over unconscious;
- individual over community;[9]
- reason over emotion;
- precision over ambiguity;
- fact over feeling;
- truth over mystery.

Increasingly, worship was reduced to a single dimension, essentially a mental activity with an emphasis on the words of the text and the rubric. This slide into one-dimensionality continued with the next development in this cultural and philosophical merry-go-round.

Scientific modernism

The Enlightenment provided the tools and the environment for the development of what we now call science. The new commitment to the application of reason as a standard approach to all problems saw an age of many new discoveries, inventions and theories. Like a mighty hurricane, science swept everything away before its path.

Like the devil in the temptations of Jesus and every political party of our age, science promised the earth. One by one, the walls of human ignorance fell before the application of reason and logic until even science itself was convinced that it could solve every problem. After Einstein and quantum physics had unlocked the most complex of creation's mysteries it appeared that there were no bounds to the application of the scientific method. Even the problems of society and the human condition would eventually be solved. Scientists were seen as the new high priests, and many basked in a confidence that they alone could make the world a better place for everyone.

This naïve confidence infected every level of human society and was only temporarily disturbed by the atrocities of two world wars. Human beings walked on the moon, giving the impression that even space is ours to exploit; new high-yield food offered a solution to the problem of human hunger; the development of cybernetics and robotics offered a glimpse of a world where humans need do only minimal work; events from one small part of the world can be seen instantaneously around the world, showing that information can no longer be controlled by even the mightiest superpower. There were, it seemed, no limits to the scientific project and most of the western world put their trust in science to create the new Utopia.

The works of David Hume in philosophy, Charles Darwin in zoology, Sigmund Freud in psychology, and Karl Marx in politics cumulatively established materialist assumptions about life and generated increasing confidence in a reductionist/scientific approach to life. The movement that got most under the skin of the Church was perhaps that initiated by Sir Alfred Ayer, known as logical positivism. His book *Language, Truth and Logic*, first published in 1936, was unusually accessible for a philosophy

book. The core of the argument would dominate popular atti-
tudes towards religious thinking for most of the century. All Ayer
did was to articulate the way that the development of science
affected people's understanding of the world and truth. His Principle of Verification suggested that if a statement could not be
shown to be true by logic or science it was either not true or
nonsense.[10] Talk of God was a particular target. Humanists took
up the gauntlet and ran with it, and religion was quickly on the
defensive. All this added further weight to the previous two
hundred years' worth of thinking that asserted the superiority of
precise reason, of logic and therefore the mind.[11]

These movements have built on each other over five centuries.
We have a society that looks for precision rather than ambiguity,
for logic rather than revelation. This has created an environment
in which worship appeals primarily to the intellect and so
reduces worship to word. It has produced a one-dimensional
approach to humanity where the language of theology is more
central to liturgy than the language of love; we end up with
worship that fails to reach the heart of the human condition.
This failure of worship has had its impact on the congregations
of the churches who are looking for something more, and they
have voted with their feet. Diminishing congregations have
brought about a lack of confidence not only in church worship,
but even in the Church itself.

Conclusions from history

I have sketched the way in which the culture of worship has
changed over five hundred years. This does not mean that
someone planning a service is necessarily conscious of it. It is
like the air we breathe. Most of the time we are completely
unaware of it. The worship planner doesn't (usually) ask him- or
herself, 'How would René Descartes have organised this service
for Pentecost?', but the subtle yet pervasive influence of these
philosophical movements has produced an environment which
largely determines a word-based approach to liturgy.

This approach is illustrated by the way we plan worship. If
you ask someone to prepare a service, 95 per cent of worship
planners will begin by considering the prayers they might use

and which readings and hymns would fit in. The beginning, and often the end point of the process, will be word-focused. Rarely does anyone begin by asking what we could 'do' in the service, what symbol might be appropriate to open up the worshippers. Our first resort is to word.

Pressure for change

If we look at the way we have tackled liturgical reform over the past forty years, the same conclusions emerge. Take, for example, the Church of England. Over the past twenty years we have seen the introduction of two new bodies of worship services. The first was *The Alternative Service Book 1980*. Beforehand, there had been twenty years of experimentation and trial to produce this alternative to the Book of Common Prayer.

Dissatisfaction with the BCP came from a number of different sources. There were those of a Catholic persuasion who disliked the essentially Protestant theology. There were those who had been influenced by the liturgical movement and the advance of liturgical scholarship in the early part of the century and con- sidered the BCP communion service to be an inadequate rite. There were the legalists who realised that many parishes were using the unauthorised 1928 Prayer Book forms of communion and morning and evening prayer. There were the modernisers who thought that the language of the sixteenth century did not help people to understand what was being said in the service. At the time new, modern-language versions of the Bible proliferated. A worship equivalent was needed.

There were many different pressure groups pushing for liturgical renewal, yet all of them saw the problem as primarily being in the words we used. Even as late as 1980 our attempts to renew our worship focused on changing the words.

The most recent liturgies of the Church of England, *Common Worship 2000*, have taken a broader approach and the need for 'liturgical formation' has become part of the current reforming agenda. Sadly, across the country the response of many Anglican clergy to *Common Worship* is one of resigned dismay that they have to go through another round of liturgical reform. I am convinced that this is because *Common Worship* is seen as producing just another set of words for services, and people are beginning to realise that altering words doesn't necessarily change hearts. The richer prose of *Common Worship* is undoubtedly superior to the language of the Alternative Service Book, which in places appeared lifeless and at times began to evoke memories of the daleks of *Dr Who*.

For the Free Churches the problems have the same root but show themselves in different ways. A more relaxed attitude towards the use of set liturgical texts may create the illusion that they are less word-obsessed. In reality they are just as word/mind-focused as the so-called liturgical Churches, if not more so. The lack of visual stimulus reveals worship that is at heart a purely mental activity. The lack of congregational text to follow creates worship that is dependent on memory – of what the preacher said, of what the prayers were about, of who was included in the intercession. Free Church worship, just as much as its liturgical sibling, needs to untangle itself from its Enlightenment origin before it can really engage with the postmodern world.

Even where Free Churches have attempted this engagement with the modern world and its new technology they often reveal their Enlightenment roots. A good example is the Willow Creek Church in Chicago.

The leadership wanted to find a form of worship that was accessible to the 'seeker'. After considerable research they discovered that most seekers want to go to church on Sunday and don't want to sing. What they produced was a Sunday event through which many thousands have been converted to faith in Christ. The model has been adapted and adopted by many churches in England as a means of making their worship more accessible, and there is much to commend it, but serious questions need to be asked about whether it is worship at all. It seems that the Willow Creek Seeker Event is no more than an expanded sermon. It is pure Reformation culture, except that the balance of power is moving from preachers with university degrees in theology to producers with degrees in information technology.

While I do not deny that language and text are important, the challenge laid before worship organisers today is not primarily about rewriting the words we say. We need a radical renewal of our attitude towards liturgy and worship, and this raises far-reaching questions about what we do and how we do it rather than what we say.

From modern to postmodern

Although each age had its counter-cultures, there was a relatively smooth progression through the centuries from the Reformation to the Enlightenment, and then on into scientific modernism. But just as the barbarians swept across Europe and destroyed the Roman mega-culture, so scientific modernism has its barbarian hordes too. They are called postmodernists.

Postmodernism not only offers a profound critique of scientific modernism but it also marks the recovery of a more holistic approach to being human. For twenty years or so we have been watching the slow crumbling of scientific certainty. As science failed to deliver Utopia people all over the globe have been discovering afresh that we are more than just a mind on legs. This is in part to do with the failure of science to deliver, but the main vehicle of postmodernism is the Internet, the twentieth-century's equivalent of the printing press.

The Internet has had a similar, yet much greater, impact on the availability of information than the printing press had in its day. At the touch of a button (or a mouse) people with the right technology can access more information than would have been imaginable even twenty years ago. There is a world of new ideas, spiritualities, theologies, politics and pleasure just waiting to be accessed. People no longer need turn to the old, wearied interpretations of life but can immerse themselves in a virtual world of new and exciting ideas and, perhaps more significantly, experiences, ranging from astrology to zoophilia via bomb-making.

As we look back on the twentieth century we see that the confidence which we put in science is misplaced. The wide-eyed optimism of the early part of the century has given way to a sense of disappointment, even despair. The three-day working week has not materialised. In fact, quite the opposite is true. Many in the western world are working far harder than they were thirty years ago while at the same time millions are un-employed and/or live in poverty. The vision of a world where everyone is fed, housed and educated has changed to a struggle to contain the pollution and ecological devastation we have caused. In spite of our amazing and ever-increasing body of knowledge about our world and universe we have still seen the proliferation and use of nuclear weapons, genocide, the rise of Communism, Fascism, sexism and the increasing trivialisation of human life in the consumer world. Science is no longer seen as being able to provide the answer.

Ecclesiastical optimists have noted the emerging interest in spirituality. David Beckham was reported as saying, 'I have a sense of spirituality. I want Brooklyn christened but I don't know into what religion yet.' Spirituality is increasingly big business on the high street and research backs up this feeling that people are more spiritually aware than they were three years ago. The Nottingham University Research into Spiritual Experiences of Those Who Don't Go to Church compares the experience of people in 2000 with the experience of people in 1987. Here are some of the figures.

	2000	1987
Detecting a pattern of events in their life	55%	29%
Awareness of the presence of God	38%	27%
Awareness of prayer being answered	37%	25%
Awareness of a sacred presence in nature	29%	16%
Awareness of the presence of the dead	25%	18%
Awareness of an evil presence	25%	12%
Cumulative Total	**76%**	**48%**

Spirituality has become big business. The number of New Age shops on the High Street are increasing. Candles, aromatherapy oils and crystals fill shop windows, and even mainstream book-sellers stock their shelves with books on alternative therapies. The failure of science has encouraged people to engage with questions that have not been asked for almost two hundred years. Sadly, though, it is not the spirituality of the Church that people are turning to.

Naïvely, it was expected by many that the sudden upsurge of interest in spirituality would bring with it a paralleled increase in church attendance, but this has not materialised. Unfortunately the institutional Churches are seen as part of the problem rather than as part of the solution. In the eyes of the postmodern seeker it is an institution clearly wedded to the old word/mind axis, and addicted to a meta-narrative that is past its sell-by date. A brief look at its worship shows this.

A pale reflection

Consider what happens when you go into a Church of England church for a Sunday communion service. I suspect the experience will be much the same for other traditions.

- We enter church and are given a service sheet/book.
- We sing something from a hymn book.
- We confess our sins by thinking about what we have done wrong and saying a prayer from the book.
- We praise God by singing or saying the Gloria.
- A prayer is read.
- We have readings from the Bible.
- A sermon is preached.
- We respond to the sermon by saying the creed.

And so it goes on. It is all on a one-dimensional word/mind axis and doesn't take into account the multi-dimensional nature of our humanity.

Take, for example, the Gloria. This is an ancient hymn of praise that almost accidentally became a fixture in the liturgy of the Church. It is there because it fulfils an important theological and human purpose. It is an act of praise to God in response to the forgiveness of our sins. We are released from guilt, so we stand (unless it is an 8 o'clock communion in which case we probably remain kneeling) and we (or the choir) sing (or we just say) – the words. Sometimes it is a rousing tune, though that is unlikely. What is much more likely is that the congregation will be expected to join in some irregular, irritating setting that was written for a choir.

Now compare this with how the world would celebrate an equivalent event, where there is something to get excited about. Imagine your football team is in the habit of winning matches.

How would the supporters celebrate this week by week? Depending on scale there would certainly be applause, probably some singing or chanting of something simple and repetitive. Some sort of physical movement – possibly dancing, maybe waving of arms, clapping above the head – might accompany this. There may be the sounding of simple instruments, pushing and swaying, spontaneous shouting of acclamation. Different cultures and subcultures will have their own variations, but the point is that it is a vibrant multi-dimensional act of praise.

I am not advocating that the Church should ape every aspect of secular praise but I cannot believe that praise of our wonderful God should be a one-dimensional, pale imitation of the way the world praises its heroes and saviours. Surely Christian worship should be richer and more dynamic than its secular counterpart? If we apply this analysis to all the elements of worship you begin to see just how one-dimensional western church worship has become – and it is frightening!

Summary

- *For the past five hundred years we have lived in a word/mind-based culture that has become the cultural and philosophical air we breathe.*
- *That culture is now breaking down rapidly but the Church and its worship is locked into it.*
- *The Church has tried to reform but has not really grasped what change is needed.*
- *If we are to begin to relate to the people of our emerging postmodern age, we need to find ways of worshipping that reflect the multi-dimensionality of human nature and move beyond the word-based mentality of the past five hundred years.*

Chapter 2

Worship in Four Dimensions

It was the era of the Toronto Blessing. Our church had been involved, yet remained a respectable Anglican distance from what we feared might have been its excesses. Many in the congregation had benefited from the ministry emanating from it so I could not be dismissive. A couple of people in particular, unrelated in any way except that they formed part of the same church congregation, intrigued me. One Sunday evening they both came for prayer and with a certain inevitability ended up lying flat on the floor, resting in the Spirit. When they came to they both related very similar experiences and showed a remarkably mature response. While resting on the floor, they both experienced intense pain; sometimes in the arms, sometimes in the legs. Both said it was as if Jesus was showing them a tiny fraction of what he experienced on the cross. They thought they were offering some kind of intercession, but were unsure how. It was as if they were standing in the gap between the suffering of humanity and the heart of God and they experienced some of his pain. At every opportunity they went for prayer ministry, and each time they had this painful experience. Yet they kept coming for prayer, again and again. It became part of their worship, uncomfortable though it might have been.

Heart, soul, mind, strength

In the last chapter I explored the way in which western popular culture developed and looked at how this affected our understanding of worship. I began to look at the changes taking place at the heart of our culture today as we move from the modern era into a new age. Because we do not know what will happen philosophers have called it simply 'postmodern'. One point is clear: the assumptions we have made about liturgy and worship in the modern era will not find much of a home in the post-modern one. I have suggested that the cultural development of the past five centuries has resulted in an over-intellectualised approach to worship. In this chapter I want to compare that approach with what I believe to be the richer and deeper appreciation of worship that we find in the Bible.

> When the Pharisees heard that [Jesus] had silenced the Sadducees, they gathered together, and one of them, a lawyer, asked him a question to test him. 'Teacher, which commandment in the law is the greatest?' [Jesus] said to him, 'You shall love the Lord your God with all your heart, and with all your soul, and with all your mind. This is the greatest and first commandment.' (Matthew 22:34–7)

I do not believe for a moment that when Jesus offered this first and greatest commandment he was presenting us with God's design for our human make-up. On the other hand, I do not think it is accidental that he pointed to these different aspects of our nature. This 'heart, soul, mind' model offers a profound critique of the temptation within the Church and western culture to see human beings as primarily 'thinking' creatures. In fact, 'mind' comes a sad last. Even in the parallel passages of Luke 10:25ff and Mark 12:28ff, with the added element of strength, 'mind' still comes a poor third. The gospel-writers are no mere secretaries, but theologians in their own right. Therefore it is likely that the order of the elements is significant. Add to this the fact that love is at the heart of the two great commandments and we see two discernable trends emerging: the priority of love over understanding; and the priority of heart over mind. This is not good news for those seeking to follow an Enlightenment agenda.

Worship is far more than mental concentration on God or intellectual stimulation. Rather it is concerned with transform-ation, not just of God's people but the whole of creation. The purpose and the effects of worship are far greater than our imagination can ever grasp, and the impact of the past five centuries has reduced not only our expectations, but also our experience of worship to a shadow of what it is meant to be.

True *weorthscipe*

In our consumer-led society a great deal of emphasis has been placed on producing worship that appeals to the congregations in our churches. Questionnaires abound. Church councils and congregations are constantly consulted. Yet our missionary situation in the western world has forced us to recognise that our worship needs to be more accessible to the non-churchgoer than ever. We have become almost desperate to draw into our worship those who find it most difficult to relate to it, and we have understandably agonised over the dilemmas that presents. In all this, it is easy to lose sight of the fact that the primary focus of worship is not the congregation, nor the world we evangelise, but God.

The first article of the Westminster Confession asks the question, 'What is the chief end of man?' The answer it offers is sublime: 'Man's chief end is to glorify God, and to enjoy him for ever.'[1] This is a surprisingly voluptuous answer given that it comes from the beginning of the Enlightenment.

Our word *worship* derives from the old English word *weorthscipe*. At a superficial level it means to give someone or something their worth. *Weorthscipe* can be offered to monarchs, works of art, even individuals. Even today English magistrates are called 'Your Worship'. This may be little more than a historical anachronism but it shows something of the way the word has evolved. However, *weorthscipe* is more than just intellectual assent to the worthiness of someone. It is more akin to the reaction of the lover to the beloved.

Weorthscipe is about giving a person their due. It is about attributing to the King of kings and Lord of lords the honour due his name. Clearly there is intellectual assent involved, but effective and affective worship must go far deeper. It is about allowing *the* Lord to be *my* Lord, like Thomas who proclaimed the risen Jesus as 'My Lord and my God' (John 20:28). This subtle transition from intellectual assent to personal commitment is of profound significance. Thomas is not satisfied with the objective recognition of the place of Jesus in the divine scheme of things or he would have declared, 'You are Lord and God'. Rather he allows the truth to inhabit him and become his own and says, '*My* Lord and *my* God'. True *weorthscipe* is entering into the relationship as well as acknowledging the truth. *Weorthscipe* is more concerned with relationship than information, more an affair of the heart than of the head.

The kissing game – *proskunein*

Perhaps the most powerful word for worship in the New Testament is *proskunein*. I remember as a young lad hearing a sermon about this. I heard the word kiss used somewhere, and for years giggled every time I heard it. I thought it was one of those naughty words teenagers look for in dictionaries – and perhaps in a way it is. *Proskunein* appears in many forms throughout the New Testament and is as rich a word as you could find. Here are some examples.

> Jesus said to him, 'Away with you, Satan! for it is written, "Worship the Lord your God, and serve only him." '
> (Matthew 4:10; see also Luke 4:8)

> [The Samaritan woman said to Jesus,] 'Our ancestors worshipped on this mountain, but you say that the place where people must worship is in Jerusalem.' Jesus said to her, 'Woman, believe me, the hour is coming when you will worship the Father neither on this mountain nor in Jerusalem. You worship what you do not know; we worship what we know, for salvation is from the Jews. But the hour is coming, and is now here, when the true worshippers will worship the Father in spirit and truth, for the Father seeks such as these to worship him. God is spirit, and those who worship him must worship in spirit and truth.' (John 4:20–24)

> And the four living creatures said, 'Amen!' And the elders fell down and worshipped. (Revelation 5:14)

In each of these passages the word used for worship is a variation on the verb *proskunein*. This is perhaps best translated 'to fall down in obeisance' or 'to approach as if to kiss'. There is something almost erotic about this verb as it underscores the quasi-physicality of true worship. There is either a falling down in awe and wonder, or a passionate embracing of God.

More than just a kiss!

This passion and intimacy is reminiscent of the word in Hebrew often translated *to know*. That word is *yada*. In this context worship is the ultimate place of coming to know. *Yada* can also mean to perceive, to discern and, crucially, to have sexual intercourse. Worship becomes the place of total inter-penetration with God – the place of true knowing – of complete intimacy and intermingling. This takes us far beyond an Enlightenment model of knowing. It peels back the layers of western philosophy and gives us a vision of a 'knowing' that touches the very depths of our humanity. Such knowing is utter submission to the God of love.

A real encounter

Proskunein, prostration before the majesty of God, conjures up other images from Scripture. Perhaps the most well known of these is the passage we usually refer to as Isaiah's call. In Isaiah chapter 6 the prophet is caught up in the presence of God and he sees the glory of heaven. His response is deeply moving. Confronted by the cherubim and seraphim, he reacts to the awesome nature of God not by praise but by penitence. Isaiah is paralysed by his own sense of sin. Compared to the grandeur of God he is nothing and recognises himself as such: 'Woe is me! I am lost, for I am a man of unclean lips, and I live among a people of unclean lips; yet my eyes have seen the King, the Lord of hosts!' (Isaiah 6:5). Here we see the response of the prophet going far beyond the intellectual, touching his deepest self.

Many see this well-known passage as a model or type for worship. It has had a profound influence on western liturgy. We come into the presence of God through an opening hymn and/ or procession together with the opening greeting, which is a declaration of the presence of God among his people ('The Lord be with you' or 'The Lord is here'). This is followed quickly by a prayer for the guidance of the Spirit through our worship. Then we are thrust into an acknowledgement of our sin and need for forgiveness.

Giving God his due – his *weorthscipe* – means allowing him

complete access to every fibre of our being, every hidden corner of our personality, every aspect of our relationship with each other, our community, our world and ourselves. We give him permission to put things right. What else would be worthy of our God?

This has become the normal pattern for the introductory rite of western worship though some are now beginning to question the long-term effects of confessing our sin as the first thing we do when we come into the presence of God.

A further insight comes from the whole assembly of Israel, gathered in magnificent array to consecrate the Temple of Solomon in 2 Chronicles 5:13–14: '[As they worshipped crying] "For he is good, for his steadfast love endures for ever", the house, the house of the Lord, was filled with a cloud, so that the priests could not stand to minister because of the cloud; for the glory of the Lord filled the house of God.'

This is a major national event. It is the equivalent of the consecration of St Paul's Cathedral or the coronation of the monarch. Suddenly the service has to be stopped because the leaders of the worship could do nothing but stand in stillness and awe. God had answered the prayers of his people and turned up. Worship leaders were so awestruck that they were unable to continue their duties. Now this may happen every week in some parish churches but it is not something I have encountered too often.

The Abba generation

Another example of the multi-dimensionality of worship can be found in St Paul's writings, where he considers the work of the Holy Spirit. One of the primary works of the Spirit is to lead us to worship God as Father. In his letter to the Romans he writes:

> For all who are led by the Spirit of God are children of God. For you did not receive a spirit of slavery to fall back into fear, but you have received a spirit of adoption. When we cry, 'Abba! Father!' it is that very Spirit bearing witness with our spirit that we are children of God. (Romans 8:14b–15)

The exclamation *Abba!* is the same word used by Jesus at the beginning of the Lord's Prayer in which he offers his followers a model for prayer. It gives us an insight and draws us into his relationship with his Father. More importantly it is the form of address Jesus uses in the garden of Gethsemane (see Mark 14:36). Here we are invited to join not only in the intimacy of Jesus with the Father, but in the very work of Jesus on the cross. This is more than a mere intellectual assent of the significance of God. It is the moulding of our will by the will of God. It opens up new horizons of relationship for the believer. This relationship gives us our true identity as the children of God. Here we see worship forming within us the reality of who we are.

A farmer's tale

Other words we could look at are *liturgy* and *cult*. Again, each points to different aspects of worship but each has its own richness. Liturgy is a composite from the two words *laos* (people) and *ergon* (work). Liturgy is the work of the people. One is reminded of Jesus' command to love God 'with all your strength', as if your livelihood depended on it. The true work of the people of God is not toiling in the fields or making furniture, but worshipping the one true God. Worship is to be that into which we pour our life's energy.

Consider the word 'cult'. In the English language it usually refers to extreme religious groups which manipulate their ad-herents. In Italian and French, though, the word still refers to Christian worship. In both countries the Eucharist is still called either *le Culte* or *il Culto*. It is a farming word having the same root as 'cultivate'; creating the right environment for fruit – in this case fruit of the Spirit – to grow, tending it with love. It carries a sense of responsibility and mutuality.

I have chosen these examples carefully but in none of them does the word/mind emphasis dominate. There are elements of intellectual assent and I am not arguing that worship has no place for the word/mind axis. What I am saying is that it must be more than this if it is to reach both its human and biblical aspirations. Note the multi-dimensionality of worship, drawing the worshipper ever deeper into the reality of God until the worshipper is transformed into his likeness. Worship is not one-dimensional but deeply multi-dimensional.

Worship *is* engagement

The New Testament does not attempt to offer us a systematic theology of worship. It has even been suggested that the New Testament is purely descriptive of the worship of the era. This would allow us to treat the New Testament picture of worship lightly. However, if the New Testament writers were theologians as well as historians, we cannot dismiss the idea that the New Testament is intended to be prescriptive about worship as well as descriptive. The pioneers of our faith offered directions about theology, redemption and ethics, behaviour, attitude towards the law and circumcision. Surely it is unrealistic to think that they offered no direction about worship. Our task is to determine which elements of New Testament teaching are intended to be authoritative for us today.

The Bible presents a picture of worship engaging the whole of our being, not just a part of it, with God. It is a total response that encompasses:

- the deepest kind of knowing;
- utter subjection to God's majesty;
- intimacy such as Jesus enjoyed;
- the engagement of our feelings and emotions;
- penitential recognition of our sinfulness;
- prostration as a physical expression of our obedience;
- physical embrace;
- hard work;
- cultivation;
- the moulding of our will by the will of God.

The Bible presents a picture of worship that goes far beyond the experience and expectation of most people in the western world.

The English are noted for our sense of reserve. We hate fuss and always stay calm. There is nothing emotional about the English. An Italian told this joke in international company.

An Englishman was staying at an Italian hotel. One evening

he came down to the bar and asked for a glass of water. 'A glass of water,' cried the barman, 'is that all you want?' And he gave the Englishman his drink. The Englishman immediately disappeared up to his room. A few minutes later he came back with the same request. The Italian barman waved his arms and protested but gave the Englishman his glass of water. This went on every five minutes for half an hour and the Italian barman became increasingly manic. Finally the Englishman came back and the barman exploded. 'What are you doing? Do you not like my drinks? Why do you just keep coming here and asking for this silly water?' The Englishman just looked embarrassed and said to the barman, 'Well, I am afraid my room is on fire!'

I did not think it was that funny but everyone else found it very amusing.

Our national character affects the way we worship and that character has influenced the nature, content and style of worship across the world through our imperialistic endeavours of the nineteenth century. English, and particularly Anglican, worship is noted for its discreet detachment; the temptation has always been that we would make prescriptive those elements of worship that sit most easily with our personality. Different groupings will face different temptations, but they are nevertheless there for all of us.

Summary

In chapter 2 I have suggested that we reduce worship primarily to mental activity and judge it by its intellectual or aesthetic appeal. I suggested that this was a product of the philosophical atmosphere that we had all breathed for five centuries. I hope to have shown that this narrow approach to worship does not match the expectations of the Scriptures, and that only by facing the full reality of worship as presented in the Bible can we begin to recapture its real impact, depth and power. It is only this worship in four dimensions – heart, soul, mind and strength – that has the power to draw the people of our world today.

Chapter 3

Transforming Worship

It was the first day of the Decade of Evangelism and the feast of the Epiphany. A new face appeared at the Sunday Eucharist. You could tell he was new to the church because he sat at the front! Throughout the service his facial expression was contorted between anguish and ecstasy. At the end of the service he explained why he had come to church. By conviction he had lived as an atheist but over the past couple of weeks he felt that he had been persecuted by evil. Sleepless nights had been overtaken by nightmares. On one occasion he thought the only way out was to try to say the Lord's Prayer. He did, and immediately the sense of fear receded. Aided by the prayers and nagging of his wife he considered coming to church. Eventually he gave in, came and sat at the front. He explained that as the service progressed he had an overwhelming sense of God's love for him personally and later in the service he committed his life to Christ. No one spoke to him, touched him or elicited any response from him, but in the process of the worship his life was radically and permanently transformed.

So far we have looked at the way worship is and how it has come to be as it is. We have looked at how worship is presented in the Bible and this gives us an idea of how worship ought to engage with the deepest aspects of our being. In this chapter we will explore the purpose and effects of worship. For some this might be obvious: it is when we 'present (y)our bodies as a living sacrifice, holy and acceptable to God, which is (y)our spiritual worship' (Romans 12:1). Worship is the act of placing before God all that we are, have been and will be.

Daring to judge

If worship is directed at God himself how do we know whether our offering is worthy? We cannot judge the effect our worship has on God – we just do not know whether God likes it or not. Since there is as yet no way of getting God to fill in a worship questionnaire or participate in a Trinitarian focus group, how can we comment critically and helpfully on our worship?

Many have used this uncertainty to present forms of worship that are subservient to their own tastes and preferences. Presumably the argument follows this pattern:

> I don't know whether God likes it;
> I may as well produce worship that I like;
> then at least one person will enjoy it!

There is a more arrogant version of this argument, which confuses my personal likes and dislikes with those of God and says, in effect, that God likes it because I do.

Through the ages the Church has used arguments like these to justify even its most esoteric acts of worship. There has been an assumption that if a service is intellectually or aesthetically pleasing then it is a 'good' act of worship. In our inability to know what truly pleases God we replace his unknown values with our human preferences. They are usually the ones we feel most comfortable with.

The Principle of Negative Reaction

We can easily fall prey to what I call the Principle of Negative Reaction. This is most clearly demonstrated when we judge worship on what it does for me, or on the basis of my/our own personal preferences. It is the spiritual equivalent of 'How was it for you, darling?' A style of worship, or even a particular service, might make us feel good, even send a shiver down the spine. The Principle of Negative Reaction, however, suggests that we learn more about ourselves and our need for growth and healing from the things we do *not* like in worship than from the things we enjoy. Those elements in worship that make us uncomfortable are more likely to reveal our immaturity, our need for healing and for growth. They more readily reveal the areas of our lives that God needs and wants to work on. Perhaps this is why reacting to congregational worship questionnaires rarely produces worship that is satisfying in the long term, because people tend to put down their likes and preferences without facing up to the real needs which can only be met by more challenging and uncomfortable worship.

You shall know them by their fruit

Our lack of certainty about the divine taste makes us feel uncertain about making liturgical judgements, but there is a way we can begin to make some judgements about our worship without resorting to merely cultural or denominational arbitrariness. Worship blesses God, but it should also bless the worshipper. Though worship is directed primarily towards God it is also intended to have an impact on us, and we can make some kind of judgement on whether it succeeds in doing so, even though this may not exactly be rocket science.

Personally, and theologically, I find it difficult to see how God can prefer one style of music to another; or one kind of service to another; but I recognise that I could be wrong. I am convinced, though, that God is pleased when he sees his people worshipping 'in spirit and in truth', or with all their heart, soul, mind and strength, whatever style is being used. The style is surely relevant only to us, not to God. What is significant is what is going on in the hearts of the worshippers. Worship that is pleasing to God must be related to the impact it is having on those who engage in it.

Normally we judge worship by cerebral or quasi-mechanistic criteria. If you are a Catholic, you may well judge the efficacy of a service on whether the ritual has been properly performed with due dignity and honour. If you are an Evangelical, it may be whether there has been a challenging sermon that led people to give their lives to Christ. If you are a charismatic, you may well judge it on how many people went for ministry or were baptised in the Spirit. But, whatever kind of human criteria we apply, they are exactly that – human. They are judgements based on our personal or corporate preferences and they create as many problems as they solve.

For example, what is dignified ritual to one may be a strait-jacket to another; a challenging sermon to one may be utterly incomprehensible to someone else; the encouragement to seek ministry in the Holy Spirit to one person may be manipulation to another. Corporate criteria might appear to be more objective than mere personal taste but even they are unhelpful expressions of preferences that offer few real clues about the true value of worship.

Formative worship

In the absence of any concrete evidence of God's preferences in worship I suggest that the criteria by which we judge the effectiveness of worship should not be the arbitrariness of our own personal tastes, nor the value-laden bases of the different strands of church traditions. We should look for signs of the long-term effects that worship has on worshippers. This will then allow us to make more objective judgements on the ultimate value of our worship and move us away from matters of mere taste. In other words we should try to see whether an act of worship achieves what is intended.

Little has been written about how we make honest and critical judgements about worship. Most liturgists restrict their explorations to the historical text and its theological implications. Students of the field of ritual studies tend to restrain their comments to the merely descriptive. Perhaps questions about whether worship 'works' are too challenging, too threatening, and open the writer up to criticism as much as anyone else. They may also encourage within us an unnecessarily critical attitude towards others, as if any more encouragement is needed among liturgists. Jesus himself warned against judgement of others and so we judge at our peril. Yet, if we are to grow in worship we need to develop an open and honest approach to the question of whether our worship works. Dare those who lead and prepare worship ask the appropriate questions of themselves, and then face up to the honest answers?

I must stress that the purpose of this kind of examination is not so that we can throw critical bombs at our theological or denominational opponents. Rather, it is to allow us to reflect critically on the worship we ourselves produce. At a sermon on Ascension Day I once heard Professor Haddon Wilmer say of politicians that they will be judged by their politics. The same is surely true of worshippers and their leaders; we will be judged by our worship.

In this chapter I will look at the impact and effect that worship is meant to have on worshippers and how we can judge whether we, as worship leaders, are achieving what God asks of us.

THREE EFFECTS

If worship is to be considered by its transforming effects on the worshippers we obviously need to ask what those effects should be. I offer three. They are that:

- worship forms the individual worshipper into the person God wants them to be;
- worship forms individual Christians into the people of God, the Body of Christ;
- worship transforms the world and the whole created order.

I will explore each of these in turn.

1. Forming the individual

Worship forms the individual worshipper into the person God wants them to be.

The Book of Revelation is not a book on which to base too much theology. Its allegory and apocalyptic symbolism make it difficult to deduce anything with certainty, yet one thing is clear: we are made for worship, and we will be worshipping for eternity. Worship is the beginning and end of our existence. These are words from Revelation 5:11–14.

> Then I looked, and I heard the voice of many angels surrounding the throne and the living creatures and the

elders; they numbered myriads of myriads and thousands of thousands, singing with full voice, 'Worthy is the Lamb that was slaughtered to receive power and wealth and wisdom and might and honour and glory and blessing!'

Then I heard every creature in heaven and on earth and under the earth and in the sea, and all that is in them, singing, 'To the one seated on the throne and to the Lamb be blessing and honour and glory and might for ever and ever!' And the four living creatures said, 'Amen!' And the elders fell down and worshipped.

The worship we experience now gives us a foretaste of the worship of heaven. All worship has this eschatological dimension. Worship on earth is meant to equip us for worship in heaven. It is therefore more than merely 'going to church'. It is the workshop where we serve our apprenticeship. It is the gymnasium where we build up our spiritual muscles. It is the place where, gradually, we are forged into the people God wants us to be. Crucially we must ask ourselves, 'Does my worship do this?'

There are bound to be parallels between worship and human nurture. There are a number of elements that need to be part of a child's life if it is to emerge as a full and responsible member of society. Children need to learn how to relate to parents. They need to be weaned from baby food to adult food. They need to learn how to speak the language of the people around them. They need to learn how to relate to others.

Similarly, worship will have a number of elements that encourage nurture. Christians need to learn how to relate to God as Father. They need to learn how to speak the language of love, of praise, of prayer. They need to learn how to be fed by the Bread and the Word of Life. They need to learn how to support and encourage others and how to be supported and encouraged by them. The content of worship should develop all these 'muscles'. Our liturgy should offer us a diet that creates the right environment for spiritual growth, forming us into the individuals God wants us to be.

Giggling, crying and healing

Sometimes this takes us into the mystery zones of our life and our faith. In 1995 the ecclesiastical world was hit by the hurricane that became known as the Toronto Blessing. Many criticised it without really trying to understand it, and certainly without experiencing it. On the other hand, many jumped uncritically onto the Toronto bandwagon only to regret it later. One of the difficulties with the Toronto Blessing, as with many other waves of spirituality throughout the history of Christianity, is that people judged it according to their own standards of taste and decency rather than ask the only question worth posing: 'Does it make people more Christlike?' When our taste is offended we tend to focus too much on manifestations and too little on epiphanies, and, as we have already seen, God's taste is always one metre beyond our grasp.

Along with thousands of others I went to Toronto to see what was happening. While there I observed one woman who outwardly appeared to be playing a game of cowboys and Indians. As the worship flowed gently onwards she skipped around the auditorium. She fired pretend arrows at some and shot guns at others. This went on for some time. Sadly, I did not have a chance to talk to her but that did not stop me musing. In play therapy this kind of behaviour is not unusual. As a citizen of a country which had seen a profound culture clash between settlers and native Americans, it would not have been surprising if this kind of behaviour had shown itself in play therapy, so why should we be surprised if it shows itself in worship, which is the place of all true healing?

During the worship I experienced some manifestations myself. Two bouts of laughter and one flood of tears left me drained and confused. I had always tried to be a person of gravitas, someone who was to be taken seriously. I tried to have a detached, philosophical approach to life. In the first years of marriage, as my wife would get more and more angry about a situation, I would often say, 'You are not being logical.' She would then respond with the supra-logical response of throwing something at me! In therapy it would have been no surprise for such a person to be put in touch with his inner, repressed self and to start to laugh or cry. Why then should this not happen in worship, the place of healing, where we are made more and more into the people God wants us to be?

At the Church of the Airport in Toronto, one major lesson for the Church was that worship is the place of healing. As people were invited to receive prayer ministry they were asked not to focus on the ministry, or the ministers, but to worship. The musicians led gentle songs of praise during the prayer time and there was a wonderful integration of worship and healing, particularly the healing of inner hurts. Sadly, much of the Church never heard this message, and some of those elements of the Church that engaged with Toronto seemed to forget the lesson very quickly.

My experience in Toronto has had a profound impact on the way I organise healing services. The opportunity to receive prayer with the laying on of hands and/or anointing forms part of the traditional rites of healing in the Church. But the key, it seems to me, is that it is properly done in an atmosphere of worship, not just where there is worship going on, but that the one seeking healing should be encouraged to worship for him- or herself. Rites related to healing are not divine magic or mechanical sacraments. Through worship the 'client' participates in their own ministry: we become the people God wants us to be.

Dreams

Similar connections can be made with dreams. Dreams appear to fulfil a number of functions and there are many theories about the way they work. For Freud, dreams bring to the mind the repressed images of the unconscious; according to Carl Jung they are symbolic representations of the personal and collective unconscious and they break open the spiritual realm that lies beyond the unconscious psyche. Whatever the truth, dreams seem to be a reshuffling of the mental pack of cards. Through the day all sorts of events and encounters impact on our psyche and leave us in some kind of mental disorder. In dreams we reshuffle them until they are back in order. Dreams bring us into meaningful contact with our hidden 'self' and therefore enable us safely to encounter and process the deepest aspects of our being.

Others suggest that dreams point to inner hurts that need

healing, or painful memories that need dealing with. Dreams provide the environment for that healing to take place. Alongside this there are those who suggest that dreams allow us the opportunity to work through realities that our conscious mind cannot bear, or that they can lead us to embrace the deepest contradictions within ourselves and become gradually more integrated people. I want to suggest that worship plays a similar role in our personal integration.

Charles Wesley ends his wonderful hymn 'Love Divine' with the assertion that our creation will be completed in heaven when we are 'lost in wonder, love and praise'. When we engage deeply with God in worship the experience has a dreamlike nature about it, and perhaps it is meant to be so. Worship can function like dream, not in the sense that it takes us out of reality into a dream land, but in the sense that it enables us to engage with reality at the deepest level. It seems that one of the functions of dreams is to enable the deeper integration of the personality. Our conscious mind is switched off by sleep and the unconscious begins to bring together the disparate elements of experience and the diverse parts of our personality, a little like the Defrag programs on PCs. They put memories and emotions in the right place on the hard drive of our being. This is a work of inner healing. If worship is the place of healing, surely it is to be expected that this integration will gradually take place deep within us as we worship.

C. S. Lewis, while commenting on the paeans of praise in the Psalms writes:

> I had noticed how the humblest, and at the same time most balanced and capacious minds praised most, while cranks, misfits, and malcontents praised least. Praise almost seems to be inner health made audible. Nor does it cease to be so when, through lack of skill, the forms of its expression are very uncouth or even ridiculous.[1]

Strange tongues
Worship seems to encourage psychological integration, and the argument becomes even more interesting if one begins to explore the relationship between praise and inner healing, or

personal integration, through the experience of the gift of tongues, or glossolalia.

Bishop Cyril Ashton[2] suggests that 'tongues is a spiritual gift with a definite healing quality assisting the integration of the personality'. He quotes Carl Jung, who suggested that tongues are an 'upsurge into the conscious of the deepest levels of the collective unconscious and, consequently . . . a help to personal integration'.[3] Professor Walter Hollenweger refers to this as the psycho-hygienic function of praying in tongues.[4]

Imagine two people, Paul and Alistair. Paul was brought up as the child of two estate workers in Norfolk. Their parents before them had been estate workers too. Paul had never done well at school, in fact he was given special needs provision in both literacy and numeracy throughout his education. He spoke with a strong lisp but had always had a lot of friends. He left school at the earliest opportunity to work, as his parents and grand-parents had before him, on the estate. He had a passion for horses and was put to work in the stables where he became an expert horseman.

Alistair was the son of a bank manager. He had done well at school but was something of a loner. He went to Oxford and graduated in philosophy before pursuing a career in law. Although brilliant with words and arguments he had never been successful in relationships and remained reluctantly single.

Both Paul and Alistair found themselves worshipping in the same congregation. Alistair had quickly been drafted onto the Church Finance Committee but Paul remained largely unnoticed. Both, through totally different stories, received the gift of tongues (glossolalia). For both it was a healing experience. Paul, not usually good at putting anything into words, suddenly found that he could praise God verbally. His voice found the words to tell God how much he loved him. For Alistair it was different but just as important. Not normally someone who showed his emotions, he would often found himself weeping as he praised God in tongues. Somehow, through this gift, he was able to express verbally his love for God.

One day, in an open meeting, Paul felt the urge to speak aloud in tongues. He did not understand this but he did what he thought was right. Out he spoke. Alistair listened, not knowing who it was that had spoken. He thought he understood what the speaker was saying. The leader asked if anyone had an 'interpretation'. Alistair began to speak, offering a 'translation' of great eloquence.

Douglas Davies[5] suggests that the use of the gift of tongues in praise and worship brings about healing in two ways: it gives a sense of personal worth to the speaker; and it breaks down the human barriers between the sophisticated and the unsophisticated. He draws on the work of Basil Bernstein[6] who suggests that there are two kinds of speech mode: *restricted* and *elaborate*. The restricted mode of speech is used within a close circle, perhaps a family or limited social group. The purpose of the language is to strengthen the group identity rather than communicate with those outside the group. The language is more concerned with heart and feelings and has a vocabulary that might only be understood by the 'in' crowd. On the other hand, the elaborate mode of speech is more formalised and communicates more highly conceptualised statements. Each phrase is calculated to convey a specific meaning to a wide audience.

A crude yet helpful distinction is that in the elaborate code, mind addresses the mind, whereas in the restricted code, heart addresses the heart. Consequently, those more used to expressing themselves in an elaborate code may well be able to participate in a philosophical discussion about whether we exist but may not know how to express their feelings. Those who more readily use a restricted language code may find it difficult to put forward an argument without emotion. Bernstein suggests that these two types of language codes are learned from the mother and that people from a higher socio-economic group are more likely to have an elaborate language code.

However, both Davies and Ashton suggest that when the gift of tongues is used, the distance between the elaborate and the restricted code users is bridged. Suddenly, the restricted code user can verbally express his praise for God in a way he previously could not do with words, and the elaborate code user can verbally express his feelings. Their limitations are overcome and each feels deeply affirmed, even healed.

Furthermore, in the public use of tongues and their interpretation the less articulate restricted code user might offer a word in a tongue and have it translated by someone who can articulate the meaning in an elaborate code. So, in worship, both find a place to participate publicly. Each contributes towards the ministry of the other. Social differences are overcome, inter-dependence is encouraged, and healing takes place within the individual, within the body of the Church and within society. This echoes the hopes and aspirations of Bill Seymour, the pastor of the Azusa Street Church whose revival in 1906 is widely seen as the fountain from which the charismatic movement of the twentieth century flowed. Bill was a black pastor of a mixed church in a time of deep racial hatred. He saw in glossolalia, the gift of tongues, the hope for the breaking down of the racial barriers in creation.

Sadly, in all but charismatic or Pentecostal worship, the public or liturgical expression of glossolalia has disappeared. Some may be relieved that this foray into one of the mystery zones of worship is not more common, but an important way of experiencing the healing effects of worship has been lost.

Whatever our reaction to the gift of tongues the basic thrust of this argument makes sense. If worship is to form us more and more into the people God wants us to be then worship and inner healing go hand in hand, and physical and even social healing may be present too.

Worship – the healing environment

Luke 13:10–17 tells the story of the crippled woman who causes Jesus double trouble. She is healed on the sabbath and in the synagogue – in the place of worship on the Lord's day! The president of the synagogue cannot believe it, and remonstrates with her that there are another six other days on which to be healed. Why should she have to desecrate the synagogue by being healed on the sabbath? It is the sort of argument most church attenders long for to liven up their services. Jesus calls the president of the synagogue a hypocrite and shames everyone. In this story Jesus re-symbolises both the synagogue and the sabbath by making them occasions for healing, pointing out not only that the synagogue *can* be a place of healing, but that it *should* be.

I was chatting to some members of an Episcopal Church in

the USA. They shared the excitement they had found in the Body, Mind and Spirit movement in the USA. They explained how it had helped them to mature as Christians and how the practice of prayer had brought them healing. Their enthusiasm was unusual for members of the fairly undemonstrative Episcopal Church. When I asked them if they had ever tried to apply their insights to the Sunday liturgy, they were astonished that such a possibility could exist. I was both surprised that they had never thought of this, and shocked that practising Christians had never realised that worship is about healing. Instead they looked outside the worship environment for styles of prayer that would help them to grow. Behind this there was the implicit assumption that worship has little to do with either encountering God or with spiritual growth.

This is not unusual. I am constantly struck by the number of Christians who seek help outside the Church in all kinds of esoteric 'spiritual' treatments for a variety of complaints without first seeking recourse to the ministries the Church has offered for centuries. This is particularly clear with healing. Two cases spring to mind. One was of a 14–year-old girl who had already grown to six feet tall and developed serious back problems. Rather than look to the healing ministry of the Church her mother took her to a so-called spiritual healer. She began to have nightmares and emotional problems. Fortunately, this encouraged her own church to take the healing ministry more seriously. Another was in a church that had a substantial and open healing ministry. One of its core members had a serious back problem and went to an acupuncturist. It was unsuccessful and the back problems continued. At no point did he even consider asking for the ministry from his church.

The Church's healing ministry is not a replacement for mainstream or alternative forms of medicine but works alongside them. Unfortunately, many Christians see the healing ministry as the last recourse of the desperate rather than as an integral element in their ultimate healing. So many of our congregations, and so many of our ministers, have little expectation that the worship and ministry of the Church can have a healing effect on their lives. Yet, as I have repeated too often in this chapter already, worship is the place of healing. This really happens, and it is one of the ways we can gain some idea of the effectiveness of our worship.

So, how do we evaluate whether an individual is personally growing and how do we know whether it is worship that is causing the growth rather than some other factor?

First, I want to suggest that we cannot make a snap judgement. We are exploring a process, not an event. It is impossible to test the impact of one service. Someone may have had a profound encounter with God, but Scripture clearly shows us that it is possible to be deeply blessed by God without there being any lasting impact, as in Jesus' healing of the ten lepers in Luke 17:12–19. We are looking for discernable signs of growth over a substantial period of time. The question to ask worship leaders is whether they see growth in the congregation they serve. Are members of our congregations becoming more Christlike through the Church's worship? Again, this is not meant to be a bomb you make to throw at someone else's congregation, but a question leaders should ask themselves with honesty and courage.

2. Forming the Church

Worship forms individual Christians into the people of God, the Body of Christ.

Worship has the potential to build community. It is about moulding individual Christians into the people of God, the Body of Christ. The New Testament lays great emphasis on the corporate nature of the Church as the Body of Christ. This is not just a theological proposition about the spiritual nature of the Church, but has practical implications for its life.

For the early Church it meant:

> They devoted themselves to the apostles' teaching and fellowship, to the breaking of bread and the prayers. Awe came upon everyone, because many wonders and signs were being done by the apostles. All who believed were together and had all things in common; they would sell their possessions and goods and distribute the proceeds to all, as any had need. Day by day, as they spent much time together

in the temple, they broke bread at home and ate their food with glad and generous hearts, praising God and having the goodwill of all the people. And day by day the Lord added to their number those who were being saved. (Acts 2:42–5)

Worshipping together strengthened their life together.

It is no accident that worship is at the heart of religious community life. For centuries religious orders have made worship a priority, worshipping together between four and seven times a day, often getting up in the middle of the night to do so. Such worship is not seen as a burden, but a privilege for those who share in it because it not only builds up their individual faith but their life together.

Chapter IV of the Rule of St Benedict echoes the words of Jesus with which I began chapter 2. Concerning the Instrument of Good Works the very first stricture reads: 'In the first place to love the Lord God with the whole heart, the whole soul, the whole strength.' This is not some pious, spiritual claim, but it has practical value. Here are two true stories that could be told again and again by those involved in worshipping communities.

Keith (we shall call him) had been a worshipping member of his church for about five years. He had managed to hold down a semi-skilled job at a local steel works. In the early 1990s, along with many hundreds of others in the area, Keith was made redundant as the manufacturing industry across the country was decimated. He found himself unemployed and almost unemployable, with a mortgage, a wife and two children to support. He was at his wits' end until two other members of his church agreed to pay his monthly mortgage. Worship had moulded them together and they knew they were part of the same family.

Andy (we shall call him) had lived with his partner for a few years and they had a baby. Andy's partner was dying and one of the ministers was called out to pray with her. She died soon afterwards. The house was a mess. The minister arranged for two members of the church to go and clean the house and help Andy get his home and his life in order. Over a number of months they helped with the housework, looked after the baby and generally encouraged Andy. He started to come to church with his daughter. Eventually he became a Christian, retrained, got a job and married. The arms of the worshipping community had reached around him and drawn him into its circle of love.

Even more kissing

The modern liturgical movement has encouraged the re-introduction of the kiss of Peace into the liturgical kitbag of the Western Church. This has encouraged better human relation-ships among the body of worshippers. It is an expression of the reconciliation that Jesus suggested in Matthew 5:23f and it seems to have taken some root in reality. Keith's and Andy's stories show the Peace being worked out in practice. They are simple examples that may be repeated in churches everywhere, or not! What they show is that worship has a practical value, that building up the Body of Christ is a reality that should flow from worshipping together.

3. Transforming Creation

Worship transforms the world and the whole created order.

The Bible makes glorious claims for the impact of worship. It suggests that our worship has a direct effect on the world, that it transforms the world. Here I am not primarily thinking about what is often called 'missionary worship', which is concerned with the style and content of worship in relation to its missionary task. The central concern of those involved in missionary worship is to use worship as a tool for evangelism. They are concerned with how accessible the worship is to the surrounding culture; whether the worship makes a direct impact on the lives of the worshippers; whether the music is appropriate and access-ible, and so on. While these are important they are not my concerns here.

Nor am I primarily concerned with the way we conduct our pastoral offices, though these can have a significant impact on our local 'world'. If we use the funeral rites effectively they can make a real difference to the bereaved and perhaps have an effect on the number of cases of grief-related depression that end up in our doctors' surgeries. Our marriage ceremonies can create a meaningful beginning to those entering this lifelong relationship and may have an impact on the divorce rate. Our baptism practice and policy may strengthen family life, especially if our baptism services can relate to the real needs of the parents. Although some of this may sound fanciful the policy and practice around our pastoral offices can form part of the transformation of the world.

Rose was a teacher and an authorised preacher in a church in Sheffield. The vicar there had recently conducted the funeral of a 17–year-old who had been found dead near some blocks of flats that were due for demolition. The flats had been a magnet for glue-sniffing and drug-taking, and Rose had herself taken reporters around the complex and shown them the glue bags and discarded syringes. The teenager's death had a profound effect on the whole community. There was a real sense that something needed to be done but no one knew what and inter-disciplinary meetings were held to explore the situation. During a service Rose had what could only be described as a vision of a huge image of Jesus, towering over the soon-to-be demolished flats with a procession of children coming out of them. They were waving their arms in the air and praising God and were followed by adults. Rose did not just enjoy the vision but allowed it to spur her and others on to work tirelessly to establish an ecumenical youth project. They raised funds and found premises to employ a full-time youth worker to work on the streets among the teenagers of that town.

Gustavo Gutiérrez, the liberation theologian, recognised that the Eucharist had the potential for 'the building up of a real human brotherhood'. He recognised that our worship should have an impact on our ethics and the way we live our lives. Rose's story demonstrates this, but even greater claims can be made for worship. It seems to me that a biblical theology of worship cannot escape the claim that the worship of the Church has an impact greater than touching the consciences of the worshippers, important though that is. I believe that there is an uncomfortable biblical dynamic that suggests our worship makes a difference to the whole created order. Awesome as it may seem, our worship might change the world.

At the time of the first multiracial South African general election in 1995, moving stories emerged of people walking for three days just to cast their vote. It was a time of great excitement, but also great fear. Informed commentators predicted racial tensions would reach boiling point, resulting in a bloodbath. To everyone's surprise no such atrocities happened. The *Guardian* carried a story of a Christian prophet who was aware of the predictions. She climbed to the top of Table Mountain and stood praying day and night, going without sleep for the whole of the election period. In a way she was the symbol of the worldwide Church praying for peace in a situation that seemed to be a time bomb just waiting to explode. Scientifically speaking we cannot know the effect that one praying prophet and a whole praying world had on that situation. What we do know is that there was no explosion and no bloodbath. What we saw was not just a lack of fighting but a profound reconciliation of races that became an inspiration to the world.

Just as God forms individual worshippers into the people he wants them to be so God longs to transform the whole of creation into what it is intended to be. We see this in the canticle, the Benedicite, or 'A Song of Creation', found in the Song of the Three:

Bless the Lord all you works of the Lord:
sing his praise and exalt him for ever.

Bless the Lord you heavens:
sing his praise and exalt him for ever.

Bless the Lord you angels of the Lord:
bless the Lord all you his hosts;

bless the Lord you waters above the heavens;
sing his praise and exalt him for ever.

Bless the Lord sun and moon:
bless the Lord you stars of heaven;

bless the Lord all rain and dew:
sing his praise and exalt him for ever.

Bless the Lord all winds that blow:
bless the Lord you fire and heat;

bless the Lord scorching wind and bitter cold:
sing his praise and exalt him for ever.

Bless the Lord dews and falling snows:
bless the Lord you nights and days;

bless the Lord light and darkness:
sing his praise and exalt him for ever.

Bless the Lord frost and cold:
bless the Lord you ice and snow;

bless the Lord lightnings and clouds:
sing his praise and exalt him for ever.

O let the earth bless the Lord:
bless the Lord you mountains and hills;

bless the Lord all that grows in the ground:
sing his praise and exalt him for ever.

Bless the Lord you springs:
bless the Lord you seas and rivers;

bless the Lord you whales and all that swim in the waters:
sing his praise and exalt him for ever.

Bless the Lord all birds of the air:
bless the Lord you beasts and cattle;

bless the Lord all people on earth:
sing his praise and exalt him for ever.

O people of God bless the Lord:
bless the Lord you priests of the Lord;

bless the Lord you servants of the Lord:
sing his praise and exalt him for ever.

Bless the Lord all you of upright spirit:
bless the Lord you that are holy and humble in heart;

bless the Father, the Son and the Holy Spirit:
sing his praise and exalt him for ever.[7]

(from Daniel 3:52–90[8])

This vision of the whole of creation being transformed as it worships God is beyond both our experience and our understanding, but we can grasp something of what is happening. Some of our experience does relate to this, and it can be called *representative* worship.

Representative worship

We are perhaps more used to this idea of representation in the context of confession. In the Book of Daniel, although the prophet is not personally guilty of sin, he kneels before the Lord God and confesses the sins of his people as if they were his (Daniel 9); he represents the people before God. He can do this because he is one of them.

The greatest act of representative confession is that of Jesus on the cross. St Paul tells us, 'I handed on to you as of first importance what I in turn had received: that Christ died for our sins in accordance with the scriptures' (1 Corinthians 15:3). He, the Sinless One, representatively took our sins onto himself. As the prophet Isaiah says, 'But he was wounded for our transgressions, crushed for our iniquities; upon him was the punishment that made us whole, and by his bruises we are healed' (Isaiah 53:5).

This same principle of representation allows us to worship on behalf of all creation, and, as we worship on its behalf, the whole of creation is being transformed into the purposes of its creator. Through our worship creation is brought to its fulfilment, and the reality of the Kingdom of God, to which our worship points, is ushered in. In this sense all worship is essentially eschatological, because it points to a future reality that we can experience now but is not yet realised in its fullness.

Some may find it difficult to believe that choral matins at St Mungo's-by-the-Style results in the transformation of the world.

But is this any more problematic than believing that my prayer for the peace of the world has any impact? Because St Mungo's is part of God's creation, when the people of St Mungo's worship then creation worships, and through them the process of redemption goes forward.

Responsive worship

Worship is primarily response: 'We love because he first loved us' (1 John 4:19). In worship we offer our loving response to the immensity of the love of God. But God doesn't just love us – he loves the whole world. Life would be so much easier if Jesus had said, 'For God so loved *the Church* that he gave his only Son.' But he didn't. He said, 'For God so loved *the world* that he gave his only Son, so that everyone who believes in him may not perish but may have eternal life' (John 3:16).

We respond to God's love on behalf of the world. Our worship, our response, therefore has a representational element to it. In a way we are responding on behalf of the universe. We represent before God all creation – our worship is creation's worship. We may not be aware of this but it is nevertheless true.

The priority of worship over liturgy

For some there is no difference between true worship and 'doing the liturgy'. Speaking at a conference for the newly ordained on the subject of creative worship, my interpretation of that title, as always, was to point out that creative worship is not about doing clever things in a service. It is about the worship leader creating the environment in which the worshipper might have a formative encounter with God. One of the group enthusiastically announced that all we had to do to see the conversion of Britain was to say the Mass properly. I admired his simple faith. But where was the evidence for this bold claim? I don't think he had thought through what he was saying or considered the many questions his statement raised. Surely, some Anglican priests had been saying the Mass properly since the Oxford Movement was born over a hundred years ago? Priests today were faithfully saying the Mass properly in empty barns of churches. Further afield Roman Catholic priests had been saying the Mass properly for centuries across the world. Surely, he just had to open his eyes to see that the mere saying of the Mass properly was leading to anything but the conversion of Britain? Either he was wrong, or everyone else had been getting it wrong for centuries.

His problem was that he was confusing liturgy with worship. This may be a matter of definition, but liturgy is not itself worship – it is a vehicle for worship. Like all vehicles it can be finely tuned for maximum performance, or it can be a clapped-out old banger that you can only trust to take you to the shops.

All worship, whether it is formally planned or not, does have a structure. All worship has a content of word and silence, action and prayer. We may not be aware of them but the structure is nevertheless there. This is our liturgy and it can either help or hinder the worship of God's people. But does it do its job? We will never know unless we are prepared to ask some difficult and possibly painful questions about its content and structure.

Does our liturgy:

- enable worship to form the individual worshipper into the person God wants them to be?
- enable worship to form individual Christians into the people of God, the Body of Christ?
- enable worship to transform the world and the whole created order?

Worship as I have described it is an affair of the heart between the individual believer and God, and an expression of the corporate love for God within the Body of Christ. Liturgy is the vehicle through which that worship is transported. So I would suggest that there are three essential purposes for liturgy.

Creative worship

Liturgy is meant to create the circumstances or environment for a formative encounter with God. Much has been said over the past few years about the relationship between worship and experience. As we increasingly move from the modern, rational world where intellectual appreciation is paramount, to a post-modern world where feeling is more important than fact, there will be an ever greater expectation that worshippers should feel something in their worship. For the past couple of decades those involved in charismatic renewal have felt the force of this expectation where worship is judged by what people have 'felt'. Worship needs to be more than just a feeling about God, but we can no longer be happy with worship that bypasses the affective areas of our personality. There needs to be an experiential element to it.

Since worship is meant to form us into the people God wants us to be, I prefer to speak of a 'formative encounter with God', rather than an experience of God. A formative encounter has the element of experience in it but it is not experience for experience's sake. Rather it is an encounter that changes and transforms us. Those elements of worship that 'form' us the most are not necessarily the ones that we directly 'experience'. The point about liturgy is that it should contain all the elements that make for complete transformation, and so aid God's worship project.

A true test of liturgy is whether it enables this transforming encounter with God, whether or not we are conscious of the encounter or the transformation. But does it happen?

Summary

In this chapter I have tried to show that the effects of worship go further than we can imagine. Sometimes worship will take us into those mystery zones of our humanity which challenge our modernist minds and disturb many of us. Yet, we must venture into these areas if worship is to have its full impact on creation and on us.

If liturgy is the vehicle through which we conduct an affair of the heart, the real question for liturgists and worship planners is how our liturgy can best do that. It is my contention that liturgy is not just about producing the right texts but creating the right environment for the people of God to engage in a formative encounter with the God they worship. This understanding of worship is a crucial concept. The 'how' is the subject of the rest of this book.

Chapter 4

Living Worship

It was my first Ash Wednesday as vicar of the parish. Using the then new order in Lent – Holy Week – Easter,[1] *we came to the imposition of ashes. All went to plan except that towards the end I felt a compulsion to pray with one of the congregation using more than just the formal words. Like a good Anglican, I resisted the urge, but wondered afterwards what might have happened had I obeyed that inner voice. The following year the service followed the same order but the imposition of ashes was different. Before we made the sign of the cross in ash and prayed the appropriate liturgical words we prayed with each person as we felt led. The effect was extraordinary. Many returned to their seats in tears. We discovered something of the power of the liturgy that lay beyond the words.*

That experience of Ash Wednesday was *the* occasion that whetted my liturgical appetite. Perhaps for the first time I realised that all I had longed and searched for in the freedom of charismatic worship was there in the liturgies of the Church. My task, as a worship leader, was to allow the inherent power of the liturgy to emerge and do its own work. I was not to be an architect or engineer of worship, but a midwife that allowed liturgy to live. Like many people of my generation I had a deep feeling that the worship of the Church was not working, but now I could see some way of putting this right. The problem lay not with the liturgy itself but with the restrictions we have put on it, its burial under layers of cultural accretions and the way we have tried to tame or domesticate it. What was needed was not

primarily revised texts (though they were needed) but a new way
to let liturgy live.

Our shop window

Public worship is where the rubber hits the road for the Church.
It is our website, our shop window and our workshop. It is where
our theology, our ethics, our anthropology, our ritual and our
spirituality all come together. It presents to the onlooker a snap-
shot of who we are. It shows whether we are a people worth
taking an interest in, and it reveals whether we relate to the
ordinary lives of individuals. It demonstrates whether the claims
we make about our God are worth pursuing or not, and in the
western culture of instant gratification, these impressions count.
You only get one chance to create a first impression, and for
most potential Christians that one chance is on a Sunday.

There is a sense, though, that our public worship is failing to
have an impact on those occasional visitors, or indeed on anyone
at all. This is even true for many Christians who come faithfully
to church week by week. Over the years we have managed to
reduce the expectations of the regulars and failed to reach out
and grab, or even just faintly touch, the occasional worshippers.

Not reaching those parts . . .

This failure has more than one simple component. A major
contributor has been the popular post-Enlightenment culture
that has infected the Church, but another factor has been the
Church's inability to relate to its surrounding culture. This came
across most clearly for me when I was on sabbatical in 2000.

I spent some time with the Cherokee. When I arrived I
attempted to contact the local Episcopal church near the community where I was working. I spoke to a senior lay person there,
to see if I could find someone at that church who could talk
about the way Cherokee spirituality related to creation. I was
shocked to be told that there were no Episcopalian Cherokee on
that particular reservation. The church only had white members.
I asked why. He suggested that the intellectual approach to the
Christian faith, typical of the Episcopal Church, did not suit

the character of the Cherokee. He suggested that the Episcopal Church was really 'God's Frozen Chosen'[2] and the Cherokee preferred 'a whoopin' and a hollarin' ', so the more emotional worship of the Baptist or Pentecostal churches suited them better.

Eventually I went to the church for the main Sunday Eucharist, where about twenty people huddled in a tiny yet charming wooden building. The style was formal and rapid, and it felt like the liturgy was there to be got through. A guest preacher gave a long exposition of the Parable of the Good Samaritan. The sermon bore no relation to the readings of the day so he began his sermon by reading the passage he wanted to preach on. It was a very quick service aimed at intellectual stimulation.

During my time with the Cherokee I found them to be a quiet people with a deep inner stillness. One of the local elders was once asked how white people could begin to appreciate the spirituality of the Cherokee. He told them to read James Mooney's *History, Myths, and Sacred Formulas of the Cherokees*[3] and then to go and sit in the forest for a day and listen to it. In an extract from my diary I wrote:

> He began by saying that silence was a key to our
> relationship with God. We do not experience silence, we
> run away from silence, because in silence we encounter
> our true selves. Silence is the place where we can listen
> to ourselves and God. The Cherokee would often just sit
> in silence – outside – and gaze at a rock, or a lake – or
> on a mountaintop. There they would meet God. God would
> speak to us rather than us speak to God. Today we are
> too ready to be caught up with our cars, or internet
> connections or whatever. Silence must be at the heart of
> worship.

The Cherokee are a people of great depth who love ritual, symbol and storytelling. Their history is one of pain, persecution and genocide, yet they never complained. They are anything but the whoopin' and hollarin' lot that I had been told about. They are a still, stoic, reflective people and it became clear that the worship adopted by the Episcopal church would never touch and move them because it did not relate to the heart or the history of the people. I later learned that most Cherokee did go to the Baptist and Pentecostal churches, because they were the first Christians to take their culture seriously and learn their language.

I could not help but reflect on how my criticisms of the American Episcopal Church could be applied to my own situation at home. Does our church worship in the culture of the community or is it just an imposed style based on some long-forgotten ideal of what the Anglican Church ought to be? Does our language, our music, our way of thinking reflect the community of which we are a part, or does it set us apart?

Speaking the language

This raises questions about the way the culture of the Church relates to the emerging postmodern culture. I have argued that most of the western world and Church still exhibits the marks of the Enlightenment and modernism, but there are signs of breaking out of this straitjacket. Most of us cannot go round with labels declaring that we are modernists or postmodernists because the influences of both have deeply affected us. Most of us have elements of modernism living comfortably alongside elements reacting against modernism. That is to be expected; we are in a transition period. That is why it is called post-modernism – because we do not actually know what will come after modernism. Each church, and even each individual, like the culture around us, is a mixture of both, but we are moving inexorably in a postmodern direction. We may not like this but nevertheless we must relate to it. Not to do so is to try to evangelise a nation without learning to speak their language, and postmodernism is the language of the age.

Anglicans and Protestants share the principle of worshipping in the vernacular, and this was also taken up by the Roman Catholic Church in 1967. It has become a principle of liturgy that people worship most effectively in their own language. Post-modernism is the language of the world today, yet the Western Church has scarcely begun the attempt to translate its worship into this new, emerging language.

To many people it has been clear that the liturgy and worship of the Western Churches is just not working. A sense of failure has been growing within the Church for decades and it has produced wave after wave of recrimination and criticism. It is in no small part responsible for the relentless revision of worship texts as the Enlightenment minds of the Church attempt to relate to the emerging culture. Unfortunately postmodernism is not looking for new words for worship but new ways of worshipping.

The best form of attack is not defence

Each strand within the Church has developed its own strategy for combating decline which in reality has been a retreat into its own conservative sphere of security. The reaction to the apparent failure of worship has usually been to revert back to what we used to do well, and try to do it even more!

- The catholic reaction has tended to retreat into ritual and unconsciously to follow the Enlightenment path of turning worship into rubric.
- The Evangelical reaction has tended to emphasise preaching at the expense of liturgy and replace worship by teaching.
- The charismatic reaction has tended to liberate worship from the restrictions placed upon it by liturgy and to have spontaneous worship led by the Spirit.
- The liberal reaction has tended to try to make the words of the liturgy more outward-looking.
- The traditionalists have tended to retreat into nostalgia, suggesting that we will never get it right until we use sixteenth-century English or even Latin as the vehicle for twenty-first-century worship.
- The postmodernists have retreated into New Age formulas, introducing candles and incense sticks at every opportunity without really understanding their place in worship.

In fairness, as each strand of the Church has offered its strategy, it has helped us focus on the real problems we face at the moment. Our wordy worship does need to recover a greater sense of the importance of the non-verbal. We have accommodated so much to the liberalising tendency of the world that it would do us no harm to ask basic questions about our call to separateness and how we can rediscover the true meaning of holiness. Worship has tended to be mere repetition and we need to find the right balance between spontaneity and order. Worship has had a

$$CHURCH \rightarrow GOD \rightarrow WORLD$$

order of priorities and this needs to be changed to

$$GOD \rightarrow WORLD \rightarrow CHURCH$$

The language of worship, in its fullest sense, is a major cause of concern unnecessarily alienating the sexes, the ages, the classes and the races. The relationship between worship and setting needs to be explored more, especially for smaller churches. There are lessons we need to learn from the secular world about the way the surrounding environment affects our emotions and enables us to have a sense of the divine in worship.

Each of these strands has its flagship churches, which are often numerically successful. There are large and growing examples, particularly in the charismatic movement. Others, seeing the apparent success of larger churches, try to copy them but rarely achieve anything approaching the growth they see in these flagships. There are literally hundreds, if not thousands of churches copying a mega-church, convinced that the answers lie in doing what they have done. But liturgy, indeed life, is not that easy.

The mega-church's size and growth is usually founded on an eclectic congregation and there is usually only room for one church of that 'type' in a particular region. Copying these churches is no answer to a local liturgical difficulty or to declining congregations. I believe that the answer to the question of how we can make worship work for us lies in an application of the lessons we can learn from the cumulative criticism of the different strands in church tradition. In a way they are all right and all have something profound to contribute.

Liturgical convergence

Over the past one hundred and fifty years or so there has been a convergence and agreement among historical liturgists about the shape, structure and content of the liturgies of the Church.

Baptism and Eucharist: Ecumenical Convergence in Celebration, edited by Max Thurian and Geoffrey Wainwright, demonstrated this.[4] It is further, and perhaps more significantly, confirmed by the experience of the laity, the people of the pews. Lay people who visit the services of liturgical churches of other denominations are often surprised by the similarity they find.

The work of the historical liturgists has been to recover for the modern Church the most ancient texts and orders of the service, particularly those of the sacraments of baptism and Eucharist. We can say with a high degree of certainty that the texts that most denominations currently use are as near to those ancient texts as we could have without sacrificing our claim to be called an authentic modern (or should that be postmodern?) Church.

There is nothing particularly praiseworthy about using ancient texts. Historicity is not of itself a virtue. But those texts did not emerge just by accident. Apart from arguing that the Holy Spirit could have been at work through the history of the development of liturgy, there is, I believe, a compelling reason why our worship today should be based largely though not exclusively on ancient forms. It is this: those forms worked for the post-Pentecost Church in providing a vehicle for worship and in creating the environment for the formative encounter with God that lies at the heart of liturgy and worship. Liturgies developed in the way they did because they mediated the presence of the Holy Spirit. They enabled the Spirit to do the work of forming individual Christians into the likeness of Christ, and forming those individuals into the Body of Christ.

The real task of worship leaders is to learn to use the liturgies we have to create the right environment for that formative encounter with God. The problem is not necessarily with the liturgies themselves, but with our inability to use them effectively.

To each part a purpose

Just as the whole of the liturgy has the purpose of forming Christians, forming the Church and transforming the world, so too each part of the liturgy has its own particular purpose.

Sometimes this is obvious, other times less so, but in the perfect liturgy each specific section will fulfil its allotted task.

Take, for example, the confession and absolution. Most services, regardless of tradition, contain some form of confession and an absolution. They fulfil a purpose, and that purpose relates just as much to our humanity as to our relationship with God and his world. The confession and absolution is about reconciliation with ourselves, the world and God.

The confession/absolution is meant to:

- bring us face to face with our sin – not just to recognise that we are sinful but to own our sin;
- bring us face to face with the consequences of our sin on ourselves, on others and the world, and on God;
- make us sorry for our sins and determined not to repeat them.

The absolution should:

- enable us to know that God utterly forgives us;
- release us into a relationship with God as Father;
- restore us to the position of real God's children;
- heal us from the effects of sin;
- heal those whom our sins have affected;
- give us the grace of God to resist those same sins again.

Those are big claims for one small part of the service! But theologically, that is what is supposed to happen when we confess our sins:

> If we say that we have fellowship with him while we are walking in darkness, we lie and do not do what is true; but if we walk in the light as he himself is in the light, we have fellowship with one another, and the blood of Jesus his Son cleanses us from all sin. If we say that we have no sin, we deceive ourselves, and the truth is not in us. If we confess our sins, he who is faithful and just will forgive us our sins and cleanse us from all unrighteousness. (1 John 1:6–9)

Sadly, this rarely happens. Instead, we rattle through the confession without even pausing for reflection after the introduction. This may have something to do with an embarrassment about sin in today's society. It may also be one of those uncomfortable parts of the service that might do us most good, but with which we are too uncomfortable to stay for too long. I think it is also worth making the distinction between having an opportunity for confession in the service order and confession really happening. It is one thing for there to be a corporate prayer to be said, or a leader offering a prayer on our behalf, but just because a confession forms part of the order it does not mean that people have confessed. We need to do more than simply provide the occasion or opportunity.

Practical, Theological, Revelatory and Formative

Every part of the service has at least three, possibly four elements to it.

At the simplest level the particular part of the service might have a *practical purpose*. Take for example, a procession. Processions can have different functions. They might be:

- a procession into Church – whether grand, with assistants, servers and choir or simply the leader of the worship going to their seat; but the practical purpose is so that the leaders can get to their places;
- a procession to the font for a baptism, where the practical purpose is to get to the place where the baptism will happen;
- the taking up of a monetary collection with the practical purpose of getting the money to the minister who will say a prayer of offering;
- an Offertory Procession bringing the bread and wine to the holy table so that it can be made ready for the Eucharist.

Behind each of these actions, which may be simple or performed with great ceremony, lies a practical purpose.

There will also be a *theological meaning*. If we continue to consider the Entry, the theological meaning might be that God is coming among his people. This may be symbolised by a cross and candles coming through the body of the congregation. Alternatively, the theological meaning might be that the people of God are coming into his presence. This could be represented by the whole congregation gathering in an ante-room and entering the Church with singing. However the entry is performed there is a theological meaning behind it.

Furthermore, there is a *revelatory possibility.* This is concerned more with what may happen in the worshipper. Each aspect of worship can be an epiphany for us if it is used creatively. If the meaning behind the Entry is that God is coming among his people, the question for worship planners is 'How can we *do* the entry so that it reveals its true purpose?' Every aspect of the service has this revelatory possibility – 'Wow, God is really here!' 'Wow, my sins really are forgiven!' 'Wow, God is the creator of all things!' There is the possibility, even likelihood, that God might show us truths about ourselves, himself and the world as we offer him our worship. The revelatory possibility is about the worshipper grasping the theological meaning for themselves.

Finally, there might be a *formative encounter.* This is when the individual worshipper, or even the whole congregation, not only grasp the meaning for themselves but experiences it so that it makes a difference to their lives. The worshipper will not merely realise that God is here, but *experience* the presence of God. If each part of our liturgy has a theological meaning and a revelatory possibility, we also need to ask ourselves how we can create the environment where those truths which we grasp with our minds can be transformed into the experience of our lives through worship. Through each part of the worship we can encounter divine love in a new way. All too often, in our planning and leading of services we have limited our understanding and expectation to the first two of these – the practical purpose and the theological meaning. Occasionally there has been the hope that a revelatory possibility might happen from time to time, but rarely, at least in the western Church have we given priority to enabling an formative encounter with God. Yet it is this that really changes lives!

Breaking it all down

At the risk of being boring I will ask these kinds of questions about the eucharistic liturgy. If you come from a church that uses a different liturgy try writing in detail what you do, and put your own questions down.

BEFORE THE SERVICE	How can we encourage people to gather, so that their gathering enhances their sense of being the people of God and heightens their expectation of God's presence?
THE ENTRANCE	How can the entrance of the ministers give the sense of God coming among his pilgrim people?
THE PREPARATION	How can we lay before God all that we have been involved in, affected by, are concerned for now, so that both they and we can be transformed by our worship?
THE CONFESSION	How can we come face to face with our sin and know God's freeing, forgiving love?
THE GLORIA	How can a song or a spoken canticle open our hearts to praise God?
THE COLLECT	How can we 'collect' up the worship up to this point to make us ready to be open to the Word of God?
THE LITURGY OF THE WORD	How can we enable the Word of God to take root in our lives?
THE RESPONSE TO THE WORD	What might be the most effective response personally and/or corporately to what we have been presented with in the Word?

THE INTERCESSIONS	How can we really engage with the world and offer prayer that relates to its needs, as well as the needs of those who are gathered?
THE PEACE	How can the Peace be a point of real reconciliation between people so that we can offer our gift on the altar with integrity?
THE PREPARATION OF THE ALTAR TABLE	How can we see the bread and wine as representing us standing in need of transformation?
THE EUCHARISTIC PRAYER	How can this be a prayer of thanks to God not just for what he has done through the history of salvation but also for what he has done for me personally and for us as a community?
THE LORD'S PRAYER	How can we say this so that we share in the dynamics Jesus intended when he gave this prayer to the disciples?
THE BREAKING OF THE BREAD	How can we share in the brokenness of Jesus, which brings life to the world?
THE INVITATION	How can the invitation be an invitation from God himself to us to share in the free gift of the life of Christ?
RECEIVING COMMUNION	How can we receive communion so that we can experience the power and the love of God which transforms our lives?

BEING SENT OUT   How can we hear the call to go, and experience the strength in which to go?

Dealing with the routine of our liturgy week by week can obscure the real point of what we are doing. Familiarity can breed contempt. By asking these kinds of questions the challenge of the liturgy is laid before us.

Expectancy violation

Worshippers need security as well as challenge. Liturgy depends for its effect on being patterned and repetitive. The repeating of an action or a prayer allows it to get under our skin. It begins to act on our unconscious as well as our conscious. Patterned and repeated behaviour allows the participants to have confidence in knowing what will happen next, and that security enables them to cope with the occasional unexpected event or 'diversion'. But in order for such diversions not to create a sense of liturgical panic they need to be in the context of a liturgy that offers security. So-called non-liturgical churches have found this, and even so-called spontaneous worship eventually falls into patterned, repeated behaviour. The Vineyard churches, so influential on the Church of England, have recognised and named its liturgical form: worship, teaching and ministry. Many Anglican churches have adopted this for their non-eucharistic services without realising that it is essentially a eucharistic format!

The Methodist hymn sandwich is an unwritten yet fixed liturgical form. I remember once being invited to take the service at my local Methodist church. When I rang the steward to ask what kind of service they were expecting, he assured me that I could do what I liked, then sent me a copy of the order of service which was set out in great detail. I wanted to change the place of the Lord's Prayer but this caused him so much irritation that in the end I did not consider it worth the effort! Looking back I cannot be too critical of him because he was merely demonstrating the human trait of needing patterned, repetitive behaviour to provide him with security.

The strength of a patterned, repeated structure to worship is that it then offers the possibility of diversion. This adds force to the novel part of the service. A friend of mine has recently undertaken some research into the relationship between music and emotion and he often speaks of the 'Principle of Expectancy Violation'.

WHAT A LOAD OF OLD CODSWALLOP!

That is expectancy violation! You would not have expected that statement there. It violates what you would have expected to happen and so accentuates the force of the point being made. The point is more subtly made using music. My friend makes the point most forcefully using the example of the well-known metrical version of Psalm 100, 'All people that on earth do dwell'. Many of us are used to singing this to the well-known tune by Bourgeois called 'Old Hundredth'. When Vaughan Williams produced his version of it, he kept the same musical arrangement as Bourgeois for the first line of the first four verses. However, the first line of the final verse changes and Vaughan Williams gives us an unexpected chord that sends a chill down the spine of the congregation who sing or hear it. This expectancy violation enhances the effect of a brilliant musical innovation.

Liturgy can use this principle effectively. However, worship that offers no sense of security will just create a neurotic and resistant congregation. Expectancy violation depends on patterned, repetitive behaviour, otherwise there is no expectancy to violate. If everything is different each time they will not be able to experience what the leader is hoping for, and they will not be able to see the real force of what is happening around them. Their minds will be focused on their own sense of insecurity. But, if handled well, it can create a tingling moment for worshippers and lead them into unexpectedly exciting encounter.

Liturgical supinity and liturgical erectitude

One of the criticisms of liturgical worship by members of non-liturgical churches is aimed at the 'no-change' syndrome. Some liturgists remain convinced that the validity of an act of worship is dependent on whether is follows certain rules or rubrics. But the problem with many liturgical acts of worship is that they contain no challenges and no surprises. There is a dull predictability about the structure, content and style, and it is this dull predictability that they are usually criticising. This is what Ronald Grimes calls *liturgical erectitude*.[5]

In his article, 'Liturgical supinity, liturgical erectitude: on the embodiment of ritual authority', Grimes suggests that there are two approaches to liturgy, an erect approach and a supine one. The erect approach is characterised by its inflexibility and the supine approach by its ability to bend itself to fit the situation. He writes:

> Liturgical erectitude is a style typified by poise and verticality. When we embody it, we stand up straight; we process with a noble simplicity. We rise above our surroundings with a quiet and confident dignity – the fruit of age, tradition, and reflection. Liturgical supinity, on the other hand, is characterized by its flexibility and its closeness to the ground. Supine, the spine hugs the earth. Supine we are integrated with our surroundings. We are attuned to them, but our openness leaves us in danger of violation.[6]

A liturgically erect approach treats the liturgy, the words and the ritual as inviolable. They are erect, rigid. I would suggest that most clergy implicitly tend to treat liturgy like this in that they follow the text and the rubric without major questioning and slot in hymns appropriately. Consequently there is little that varies from week to week apart from the liturgically suggested seasonal material. There is little that bends to the local situation. I would also contend that it is this liturgical erectitude, whether conscious or unconscious, that has led us to the current position in which our worship lacks the power and the vulnerability to touch the world in its weakness.

There is a story (I do not know whether it is true) that in 1917 the Russian Orthodox Church was holding a synod in the same street and at the same time that the Russian Revolution was starting. They were discussing the colour of vestments and refused to break into their discussions to take note of what was happening outside. True or not, this demonstrates liturgical erectitude at its worst.

Supinity, on the other hand, allows the liturgy to be 'bent' by local culture, events, moods, custom or personality to fit the situation.

If Grimes is right, and I believe that he is, the task of the worship planner is to draw out of the liturgy the power that is already there to transform people and situations. I am not advocating a worship free-for-all, but rather a creative approach to liturgy that leads the people of God to an encounter with the one whom they worship and adore.

Summary

In this chapter I began with the assertion that liturgy has its own inherent power, and that the task of the worship leaders is to let liturgy live. This means that:

- *it must relate to the culture around it and 'speak the vernacular';*
- *we should progressively peel back the layers of irrelevancy that have been heaped upon it;*
- *we should find ways to allow each part of the service to fulfil its own task;*
- *it should not be seen as 'fixed in stone' (erectitude) but should be moulded around the lives of the worshippers (supinity);*
- *it should lead us to a formative encounter with God.*

In this way our worship can become a living, dynamic entity that takes the offering of our lives as its raw material and transforms them into something beautiful for God.

Chapter 5

Parabolic Worship

I was very nervous. It was my first real meeting with one of the Cherokee elders, Gerry, and I was keen to make an impression. Gerry was older than I anticipated, in his 70s, but he was warm towards me. He asked me what I wanted but the more I spoke, the more tongue-tied I became. My nerves were getting the better of me and I felt a little foolish. I tried to explain why I thought that symbols in worship were like keys that opened up the deepest elements of our humanity to God, but it all felt confused. There was a silence, then he spoke. He told me a Cherokee story of a stickball game where the animals played the birds. I then asked another question, and he told me a story of how the Little People protected a gorge. And he kept going, telling me story after story after story. I felt annoyed. I had asked a perfectly simple question, and there was no need for him to go round the mountains to avoid the answer! But unusually for me, I was too polite to say anything.

A storytelling culture

I discovered that storytelling is a major feature of Cherokee life and I quickly realised that whenever I asked Gerry a question he would tell me a story. As time went by, I realised that this always happened, whoever I talked with at any depth. No one ever gave me a stock answer, but they almost always told a relevant story. In Cherokee culture, answers tend not to come as statements, but as stories.

Stories differ quite radically from statements. By their very nature, they allow several interpretations. They are polyvalent: there are many ways of understanding them. They allow the hearer to engage with the subject at his or her own level. It matters not whether you are a child of five or a university professor of literature; there is something that everyone can get out of a story. We take from the story what is relevant to us at that particular time rather than what the speaker wants us to hear. We therefore bring to the story all our experience: our history, our expectations, our needs, our inner longings and our own personal search for truth.

As the poet W. H. Auden wrote, 'You cannot tell people what to do, you can only tell them parables, and that is what art really is, particular stories of particular people and experiences, from which each according to his immediate and peculiar needs may draw his conclusions.'[1]

Storytelling as an educational model

I spoke with the Education Director of the Cherokee Museum, who had collected many of the stories that the Cherokee tell and had a particular interest in storytelling.[2] She explained to me that when the Cherokee tell a story it is not merely a telling but a re-creation of the Cherokee life. In the telling of the story the life of the people is passed on. Therefore storytelling has an essentially religious dimension to it.

In storytelling the individuals learn more effectively, because they take from the story that which relates to their own personal circumstances. This is an effective application of the adult education dictum that *people learn what they want to learn.*

Storytelling also functions as a means of passing on wisdom and practical life skills. For example, when a Cherokee sees a strawberry they will automatically think of the story about where the strawberry came from. This is a story about reconciliation between man and woman.

> One of the ones [stories] that I like to tell to people here, and through my storytelling I've tried to sort of analyse what the stories really meant when they were presented to the children back in the old times. And I've found specifically that stories like the story of the creation of

strawberries have special meanings, and I'll try to convey that.

They say once there was a man who, in this matrilineal society, his wife had told him to go out and kill a deer that day. And he went out with good intentions of bringing back a deer, because her family coming that evening to have dinner with them, and the grandmother, her mother, was a very important person in that society.

So he went out that day and he was looking for a deer, preferably the best one he could find. And he happened to come across a fellow who had fallen into a ravine and his leg was broken, and so he went down into the ravine and helped him out and carried him back to his village, and by the time he made it back to the village, it was very late in the day.

So he went back into the forest real quickly and started to hunt. And by that time all of the deer had gone in and he couldn't find one. So he came back to the village where his wife was living. And she saw him coming on the hillside. And he didn't have a deer. So she got very angry and she began to throw things, and she ran away out of the village and left and went back to her own village, her mother's village.

And he came back and was praying to the Great Spirit and was telling him that he would like for the Great Spirit to slow her down so that he could tell her what happened that day and the reason for him not bringing the deer back.

She was moving very quickly, and the Great Spirit said that he would. So he began to put beautiful flowers in her path. And this didn't slow her down at all, she just kept right on running as fast as she could go. And so he began to put fruit trees in her path, and she would go round them and was not even interested in the fruit.

So the Great Spirit said that he would have to put something in the path that smelled delicious, that looked beautiful to the eye, and tasted very, very good. So he put this little plant down near her feet, because she was angry and looking down. And she saw these beautiful little white flowers, and then began to see a red fruit on the ground. Then eventually she smelled it, and it was wonderful. And then she began to pick some of them and taste them, and they were so good that she sat down in the middle of the patch.

And the young man caught up with her while she was eating the strawberries, and he apologized to her and told her what happened. So she realized that she had left in anger and went on back to the village.

I think this is a teaching to children that we shouldn't in the heat of anger jump up and run away and make real drastic decisions or actions at that point.[3]

When the storyteller tells the story to those getting married, or those who are married, he ends by saying simply, 'so if you want a happy marriage keep something strawberry in your kitchen'. This is not magic, or superstition, as was thought by the first Christian missionaries. Instead the story is an effective way to remind a couple of a truth, and the strawberry becomes an effective sign in nature to remind the couple of the need for constant reconciliation in the marriage relationship. It is at this level that many of the Cherokee stories function. This kind of storytelling integrates their lives with their environment, and nature itself becomes the library of the tribe's collective, practical wisdom.

The western approach

Although storytelling is slowly gaining acceptance in western European culture it is still more a part of the world of entertainment than education. The western approach to education is quite different. Primarily it is the passing on of information from one person to another. There is a teacher and a student, and each knows their place in a hierarchical structure. We are used to making a statement or presenting an argument rather than telling a story.

One of the difficulties we face lies with the nature of stories themselves. We tend constantly to try to work from mystery and ambiguity towards fact and explanation. By definition stories are open to a multiplicity of meanings but in western society we are ill at ease with ambiguity. Our minds find it difficult to cope with the reality that there may be more than one interpretation of a statement and instead try to assert the veracity of one answer over another. We have been trained this way; our culture forces us into this mould. I remember that when we began to do simultaneous equations at school, I was initially baffled that *one* equation could have *two* or more answers at the same time. My head told me that there should only be one solution to an equation. It wasn't until I made a conceptual leap that I could cope and move on to understand how they worked.

When we ask a question, we expect something approaching a straight answer, and usually that is what we get. That was what I expected from Gerry. When I am asked a question I return with a statement of my point of view, or offer the questioner the benefit of my wisdom or experience (usually whether I have any wisdom or experience to offer or not!). It is *my* answer which I give. My expectation, or at least my hope, is that the listener will take it on board, and be convinced of all my arguments. I declare what I believe; it confers upon me a certain honour. It is as much about power and control as about the sharing of knowledge.

Our theology reflects the cultural environment in which we grow. As I have suggested in chapter 1, since the Reformation theology has tended towards precision, and likewise liturgy. Theology is an arena of argument. Over the past five hundred years the dialectics between Protestant and Catholic, and between theologians, have made the tools of theology very precise and very directive. There is little room for the polyvalence of storytelling.

Of course there have been dissenting voices advocating a more indirect style of theology (Kierkegaard, Bonhoeffer and Tillich, for example) but most theology is of its time and tends towards modernist, unambiguous conclusions. The late John Tinsley wrote a well-known article called 'Tell it slant'[4] in which he argued that theology by its nature should tend towards ambiguity, but he also recognised that this is far from the truth of the situation today.

All this is very different from the storytelling cultures of the Cherokee and others like them.

The Big Match: storytelling v statement-making

The differences between a storytelling culture and a statement-making (or directive) culture are vast. In a storytelling culture the responsibility is on the hearer to listen and learn. In a directive culture the emphasis is on the statement-maker to propound 'the truth'.

By placing the emphases of each alongside the other we can begin to see the different way in which each culture works.

Storytelling	Statement-making
teller offers a story owned by the community	speaker owns what he or she says
shares community wealth	imposing one view
listening is key	telling is key
encourages personal engagement	receives what the speaker offers
aims to have many levels of understanding (polyvalent)	aims towards clarity and lack of ambiguity (unambiguous)
story is generally non-directive	statement is directive
aims to encourage the hearer to engage	aims to persuade
non-hierarchical	based on a hierarchical structure
responsibility is on the hearer	responsibility is on the speaker
relates to the listener's life	relates to the speaker's life
listener engages at listener's level	listener engages at speaker's level
listener is in control	speaker is in control
relates more to personal experience	relates more to objective facts

Although I have put the values and emphases of each culture side by side I do not want to suggest that one is better than the other, but that each has a different function. There are lessons that each approach can learn from the other and each style may be more appropriate in one context than another. For example, if someone needs to build a house it would be more useful to offer them a few simple tips on engineering than to tell them the story of the three little pigs. If, however, you wanted to encourage someone to base their living on solid principles, Jesus' story about the wise man who built his house on a rock rather than a sand foundation (cf. Luke 6:47–9) would be much more helpful.

A storytelling approach has pastoral advantages. As a minister who conducts funerals I am often faced with the questions, 'Why does someone so young have to die?' or, 'Why did such a good person die?' or some other relevant articulation of the problem of evil. We have no compelling answers to those kinds of questions, but we do have a compelling story, that of Jesus and his death. What would happen if we tried less to appear to be clever in giving the right answer and instead tried more to be humble in telling an appropriate story? After all, isn't that what Jesus did?

Jesus – storyteller *par excellence*

Because the gospels are not biographies there will always be an element of uncertainty about drawing hard and fast conclusions about Jesus' teaching method. One thing we can say with a high degree of certainty is that he was a storyteller. This comes across strongly in the first three (Synoptic) gospels, though less so in John. Here we see a comparison between the primarily story-telling approach of the Synoptic gospels and the more directive mentality of John's gospel. It is interesting to speculate what might lie behind this difference in approach.

Although the first three gospels have their own particular theological slants, they are essentially stories told to keep the reality of Jesus alive. The Synoptic writers are first storytellers, and only secondly theologians. With John's gospel we see things the other way round. While John's gospel clearly presents the story of Jesus it seems the writer is first a theologian and only secondarily a storyteller. This shows in the way Jesus is presented. The 'I am' sayings are the antithesis of the story approach of the Synoptics. The writer of John's gospel appears to have a greater urgency to make theological statements about Jesus and so replaces Jesus the storyteller with Jesus the master debater.

Stories must have been important to Jesus. The parables form approximately one third of his recorded teaching and it would appear they provided his preferred method of teaching. One of the most famous, the Parable of the Good Samaritan, is prefaced by a question from the hearer to Jesus.

> Just then a lawyer stood up to test Jesus. 'Teacher,' he said, 'what must I do to inherit eternal life?' He said to him, 'What is written in the law? What do you read there?' He answered, 'You shall love the Lord your God with all your heart, and with all your soul, and with all your strength, and with all your mind; and your neighbour as yourself.' And he said to him, 'You have given the right answer; do this, and you will live.' But wanting to justify himself, he asked Jesus, 'And who is my neighbour?' Jesus replied, 'A man was going down from Jerusalem to Jericho . . . (Luke 10:25f)

Jesus refuses to give a direct answer to either question. To the first question he replies with another question, 'What is written in the law? What do you read there?' In response to the supplementary question he begins the story.

In another famous parable, the Parable of the Prodigal Son, Jesus is again answering, this time, a criticism: 'And the Pharisees and the scribes were grumbling and saying, "This fellow welcomes sinners and eats with them" ' (Luke 15:2). He then goes on to tell the Parable of the Lost Sheep, the Lost Coin and then the Lost Son!

I am not saying that Jesus never gave a straight answer, but the storytelling culture was the one he seemed to prefer in leading people to a deeper knowledge of themselves. Jesus' primary method of teaching appears to be largely non-directive, which could be called 'parabolic'.

Storytelling and worship

The word 'parable' comes from the Greek, meaning analogy or comparison. It is a story that makes a point by suggesting something else. But I would also like to use its mathematical implications here too. A parabola is an open-ended curve based on a plane taken from the cross section of a cone. A parabolic curve moves around a fixed point, the focus. What is significant for me is that a parabola moves around the focus rather than hits it head on. It is also open ended.

'Interesting,' I can hear you saying, 'but what on earth has this got to do with worship or liturgy?' A key question, it seems to me, is which of the above approaches is more appropriate for worship. For centuries in the Western Church our worship, as well as our theology, has had more in common with the directive approach than with storytelling. I suggest that an approach more akin to storytelling holds more possibilities for worship in a postmodern age primarily because of the subject matter it deals with, namely our humanity in relation to God.

Parabolic liturgy

The western approach to liturgical texts is to treat them in a linear, directive way. I suggested in chapter 1 how, during the Reformation and beyond, worship, and particularly the production of liturgical text and rubric, had taken on a theological rather than a liturgical methodology. An affair of the heart had become a process of the mind.

Worship, and particularly preaching, has been seen as a way of passing on information about the Christian faith or exhorting people to behave in a more Christian way. Liturgical texts are written so that the listener will be theologically educated by osmosis, rather than spiritually formed by the Holy Spirit. Most worship in the West is organised so that either a particular 'leader-led' response is encouraged, even manipulated, or the president leads in such a way that no response is allowed at all. Either way the leader, or the president, is the one in control.

So often our worship presents the story of the Church, or the story of salvation history through Jesus, while paying scant regard to the personal circumstances of those who make up the major part of the worshipping body. Because of the way liturgy is written and produced we are asked to engage with worship at the level of the liturgist rather than the participant. The liturgy of the Church is often more concerned with presenting the objective truth about Jesus than recognising the personal realities of the congregation and helping them to cope with them.

Parabolic worship

Worship is not the presentation of the facts of the faith in a neat educational package called the liturgy. Sadly, though, the worship of the Church is often celebrated that way. Instead, it is the offering of the people – heart, soul, mind and strength. We give ourselves to God and so are transformed in his will. Worship is about transformation, not education and it is conducted in the context of a dynamic personal relationship rather than a hierarchical structure.

The subject matter of worship is the lives of God's people, therefore my contention is that our worship today needs to be more like storytelling than statement-making. What I want to develop is the liturgical equivalent of storytelling – parabolic worship.

What does this mean in practice for worship? What would parabolic worship look like? I suggest that it might be worship where:

- presidency/leadership is invisible;
- presidency/leadership is based on what is happening among the people, not what is written on the service order;
- personal encounter with God is the expectation and the assumption of leaders and people;
- each person can offer his or her own life for transformation and there is the opportunity for this to happen;
- storytelling, symbol and active response are common features;
- the worship is polyvalent;
- each element of the liturgy fulfils its function and this is experienced by the congregation;
- each person can enter into the dynamics of worship at a level that is appropriate and real for them;
- each member of the congregation is encouraged to take responsibility for their own formation;
- the leadership is not directive but allows freedom to the worshippers to react or respond in whatever way is appropriate for them individually;
- there is listening to God rather than the directions/exhortation of the leader;

• worship is more than words.

All these have far more in common with storytelling than with the linear, directive approach so embedded in western worship and culture.

Although Christ is the Word of God, he refuses to be imprisoned by mere words. Christ is always beyond words, so it is no surprise that our worship needs to reflect this. It is the arrogance of post-Reformation theology that sees worship as a vehicle for theology, even though this is an impossible task. If Jesus as Christ himself is always beyond words our worship of him must go beyond words too. Our worship can never remain linear and directive. If our worship is to be worthy of the God we adore, it needs to become increasingly parabolic and in doing so give a greater space for God to do his work.

Summary

I have suggested that storytelling presents us with a new model of formation. It creates an open future rather than following the linear approach of western science. Jesus used parables as a major tool in his teaching ministry and we ought to learn from that. I believe that worship itself should be more akin to storytelling and become 'parabolic'. In doing so we give God more space and freedom to do what he wants with his people in worship, and maybe we even begin to discover what it means to worship Jesus' way.

Chapter 6

Symbolic Worship

At an ecumenical service to celebrate Pentecost, intercession was offered by inviting people to place grains of incense onto hot, glowing charcoal in a large brass bowl in front of an icon. Each time incense was placed on the hot coals a puff of smoke would ascend from it. It was explained that this is a biblical way of praying and that the ascending cloud of smoke symbolised our prayer rising to the heart of God. Beforehand there was some concern that the Free Church people would not like it. They did. In fact, the most enthusiastic seemed to be the members of the Salvation Army, and people queued patiently in long lines to offer their prayer. One person waited carrying a small dog, which gave a number of us real concern – until he dropped his grains in the bowl and then moved off to pray on his own (well, with the dog) elsewhere in the church!

Praying aloud (or should that be 'allowed'?)

My experience has led me to conclude that people respond more freely and more deeply to a symbolic representation of the love of God than to a verbal presentation from a leader. This seems to be true regardless of churchmanship or spirituality.

During my formative period as a Christian I was part of a student prayer group that both blessed and distressed me. It blessed me because the group's faith, prayerful spontaneity and freedom encouraged me. It distressed me because I never really felt able to share as fully as I would have liked in the open prayer that was at the heart of the group's life. I would spend most of the meeting desperately trying to work out what to say. It would take me so long to pluck up the courage to say it that it felt anything but spontaneous, but fortunately only I was aware of it! I struggled with this tension of knowing what to say yet lacking the confidence to say it for so long that I was usually foiled at the last minute by the leader suggesting we should close with the Grace. I can still feel those conflicting emotions of frustration at not being allowed to pray yet relief at not having to. At the time I was convinced that there must be something wrong with my relationship with God because I never felt as comfortable with open prayer as other people seemed to be. Eventually I did get used to praying aloud and my discomfort quickly disappeared. But every time I try to encourage others to share in open prayer my student apprehension floods into my memory. I try to be sensitive to people's inhibitions because I can remember my own. I try to encourage people, so that they, like me, might be able to overcome their spiritual shyness.

In my first church as vicar this tactic seemed to work reasonably well. Certainly the more extrovert Christians managed to launch into open prayer with differing degrees of confidence, and eventually praying aloud became normal. However, towards the end of my time in that parish I began to wonder if the ability to participate in open, spoken prayer was more a function of personality than spirituality.

'Doing' prayer

In my second church I tried the same kind of tactic, but praying aloud seemed a lost cause. It was for that reason that we started using prayer candles. Rather than exhorting people to pray aloud, with the result that those who could not felt guilty, we tried to encourage people to 'do' prayer rather than say it. At first this meant lighting a candle, putting a fish in a net, placing a stone in water, or leaving an article at the altar. As we moved away from an expectation of, and dependence on, words people were released into prayer. We bought a prayer candle stand that held 32 candles. Now 50–60 candles are lit at any one time and another stand has been provided.

These 'enacted' prayers are not new ways of praying, but by moving away from word-based prayer people have been able to participate in greater numbers and, I believe, greater depth. If we had invited open prayer at that ecumenical service ten or a dozen people might have shared in the prayer. Two hundred active participants would have been both unthinkable and unsustainable, but that was the result.

In this and many other examples, the transfer of emphasis from words to symbolic action is significant, and there are a number of reasons why this is so.

Passive laity

Many members of our congregations do not feel actively encouraged in church. For decades, perhaps even centuries, the Church has deskilled its laity, and not recognised the significant roles and responsibilities people carry in the wider world. Robert Warren, formerly the Church of England's National Officer for Evangelism, tells of a situation where a clergyman introduced a member of his congregation to the visiting bishop as the church's head server, omitting to mention the fact that he was an executive of a regional health authority. Only recently have lay people been encouraged to have a role in the life of the Church that was vocal rather than unspoken. Instead, Western Churches have developed hierarchical structures that have elevated the theologically educated priesthood above the practically educated laity. The need of clergy to control their congregations is not conducive to active involvement in the Church's ministry or to real freedom in prayer.

For this reason, I also suspect that many lay people do not feel verbally or vocally confident in church. A tradition has developed in many churches that the minister or the priest does everything. The story of the Devon minister who asked one of his leading lay people to read the Scriptures only to be told in no uncertain terms, 'But that be your job, Vicar!' is not uncommon even in the Church today, and it expresses a deep-seated attitude among many churchgoers. Lay people are supposed to be silent, and so they remain.

A verbally challenged culture

Our culture adds another dimension of inhibition. We live in an increasingly visual age rather than a verbal one. Television has replaced the radio; PowerPoint has replaced the OHP acetate;

DIY instructions are often given in cartoon rather than written format. In this kind of culture it is understandable that people might feel inhibited at having to make a verbal response to God.

A solely verbal response to anything in normal life is a rarity nowadays. A normal reaction to any human situation would be focused on a hug, a tear, a kiss, a handshake or a similar action. Words may well accompany the action but they are secondary, merely supporting whatever the physical expression may be.

The power of symbol

Northern Ireland is well known for its troubled past. There have been many meetings between the British Prime Minister and representatives of the dissident republican movement. The two sets of leaders would exchange greetings but, as a matter of policy, the British Prime Minister would never shake hands with those who were considered the representatives of terrorists. The handshake, or lack of it, was the telling action in the encounter. When they finally did shake hands during the talks that led up to the Good Friday Agreement the pictures were flashed across the world and dominated the front pages. Actions really do speak louder than words. It is said that if you chop the arms off an Italian you render him speechless. Even our normal, everyday speech is accompanied by gesture, so it is no surprise that people struggle when they are expected to make a purely verbal response in a church context. People are being asked to behave in an unnatural way, so initial reticence should be no surprise.

A person's ability or inability to participate in verbal activity in church depends on factors that have little to do with their spiritual maturity. This is particularly true of people with an introverted rather than an extroverted[1] personality type. All the external pressures inhibit participation in open prayer.

I am not criticising open prayer here. I have been blessed by it, am encouraged by it, and want to encourage other people in it. However, there are negative influences that come into play as soon as we make this the normal form of prayer. There are also positive reasons why we should have a greater respect for the non-verbal or symbolic response.

'Enacted' prayer

Enacted prayer is holistic because it allows us to use our bodies and more. Lighting a candle or dropping grains of incense onto charcoal gives us permission to respond physically, as well as verbally and mentally. For many this greater use of the whole person in prayer may also unlock a person's willingness to engage emotionally and spiritually too.

'Enacted' rather than spoken prayer offers greater freedom to those who pray. If intercessions are spoken, only a limited number of people can actively engage with them and only a limited number of prayers can be articulated. We all may need to grow in our understanding of representative and corporate prayer, and how to engage with prayer when we are not actively involved, but this kind of enacted prayer allows the maximum number of people to participate at their own level, in their own way, regardless of personality or maturity. Everyone is equal.

A person lighting a candle offers the concerns of his or her own heart and so actively shares in the corporate act of praying. They feel that their concerns are heard and so are affirmed in their relationship with God. Enacted prayer allows people to enter into the prayer at their own level without embarrassment.

A friend of mine wanted people at a conference to pray for the young people who had left the Church since 1980. The numbers concerned were astronomical. Instead of just telling people the numbers he collected some dried beans, roughly one for every lost young person. As the prayer began he threw the sack of beans onto the conference floor. They spilled everywhere. The point was made and the prayer that followed was powerful.

Polyvalence

Polyvalence is the key! This kind of liturgical act has many parallels to storytelling. In the last chapter I suggested that some of the marks of storytelling are that it:

- encourages personal engagement rather than receiving what the speaker offers;
- aims to have many levels of understanding rather than aims

at clarity and lack of ambiguity, i.e. it is polyvalent rather than unambiguous;

- is generally non-directive;
- encourages the hearer to engage rather than to persuade;
- relates to the listener's rather than the speaker's life;
- engages the listener at his or her level;
- relates more to 'personal' than objective truth.

These are all as true of symbolic action as they are of storytelling and as such they provide an effective foundation on which worship can be constructed. Their importance to parabolic worship lies in their polyvalence, the fact that they are open to many different interpretations.

This polyvalence can be seen as a weakness as well as a strength, and many treat it that way. Particularly since the Reformation, words have tended towards precision and, particularly in Protestant circles, there has been a tendency to be cautious of the use of symbols precisely for this reason. This suspicion is rooted in the belief that symbols are at best an unnecessary distraction from the real concentration of worship. There is also a deep concern that the meanings conveyed by symbols are less controllable. Trying to control the theology of symbol is like trying to herd cats.

A theoretical interlude – levels of interpretation

Larry Hoffmann took some of the ideas of the sociologist Peter Berger and applied them to ritual and ceremony. He suggested that ritual action and symbol in worship have four different layers of meaning.

PRIVATE LEVEL   What the symbol means to the individual.

PUBLIC LEVEL   Where there is some corporate or congregational consensus about what is happening.

OFFICIAL LEVEL   What the authorities say the meaning is.

PARADIGMATIC LEVEL   Where the meaning is given by its outcome, or how it moves us or affects us.

Two examples
Baptism

Consider baptism as one example. Although different Churches have different theologies of initiation, at most baptisms there are a number of things going on that go far beyond what a particular Church teaches about baptismal regeneration in Christ.

At the *private level* the parents might think that they are bringing their child for baptism because it will mean that, if it dies, it can go straight to heaven rather than go to 'limbo'. At the *public level* the congregation may share a wider community view that children who are not baptised are unlucky and so shouldn't be allowed in other people's houses until they are baptised. At the *official level* the Church teaches that baptism is about being a member of the Church and incorporation into Christ. At the *paradigmatic level* a parent might feel so unwelcome at the church that they would never think of going back until the next child comes along.

Mothering Sunday

Consider a Mothering Sunday service. In the UK this happens on the Fourth Sunday of Lent. Many churches give a small bunch of flowers to all the women at the service, regardless of whether they are mothers or not. How might these events be interpreted?

At the *private level* there may be present a person who is emotionally disturbed because they had an abusive mother, or a mother who feels profoundly guilty about giving up a child at birth. At the *public level* the community is saying 'Thank you' to all mothers for the sacrifices they make in bringing up their children, and it is a special day for the Mothers' Union or other similar organisations. At the *official level* the Church is explaining that the true mother here is the Church and that Mary is the model of motherhood. At the *paradigmatic level* the person who was upset because they had an abusive mother experiences healing in that relationship and so no longer acts out of that pain, or the mother who gave up her child at birth finds a sense of forgiveness.

Hoffman is not concerned with *what* the interpretations are but *how* the symbols are interpreted differently, but we can see how these different levels of interpretation work. He argues that all four of these levels are in operation when any ceremony or ritual is performed in worship. We cannot remove the private interpretation by reinforcing the official one; they all operate at the same time and if we want to be aware of what is happening in our services we need to take account of these different levels of interpretation.

Another example of how the same activity can have different meanings for different people can be seen in a comment about how the priest, in many churches, has his or her hands washed just before the eucharistic prayer. The official meaning relates to the purity of the priest before he or she presides at the eucharistic prayer. However, one day, a member of my congregation spotted this particular ritual for the first time. At the end of the service he asked, 'Why did you do that Pontius Pilate thing during the collection hymn?' The private interpretation was the opposite of the official interpretation. You could point to his ignorance or the lack of teaching in the church concerned, but I would suggest it demonstrates just how conscious we need to be about the way people interpret the actions we perform and the ritual we use, especially the ones we are not even aware of.

Polyvalence – opening new doors

Some have seen this multi-layered meaning as a reason to avoid, or limit, the use of symbol and action in worship, because they can never be contained within their official, theological meaning and are always ready to burst out of the confines of the tombs in which we try to imprison them. While theologians will always want to limit the potential meaning of symbolism by telling us that *this* is what they mean, Hoffmann pricks their bubble by asserting that there will *always* be the four levels of interpretation. We cannot stop it happening simply by shouting the official meaning more loudly than the others. Polyvalence is here to stay. To those who want to control or limit the communicated meaning in an act of worship this is a dangerous prospect. Yet it is this variety of interpretation, this polyvalence, which gives this kind of symbolic action such exciting possibilities. It opens up new horizons for worship and for the worshipper.

The use of symbol and symbolic action can liberate worshippers into encounters with God in new and personal ways. It takes control of what does or does not happen in worship out of the hands of the leader or the church authorities. Just as the Reformation liberated the use of Scripture so that people could read, understand and interpret it for themselves, parabolic worship offers a new reformation, liberating people not into Scripture but into a personal encounter with God through worship. Rather than a symbol's lack of precision presenting a problem it opens up new opportunities. The fact that symbols can be interpreted in many different ways allows each individual to respond personally and subjectively while sharing in the same corporate worship experience.

Imagine a situation where two people are in a church congregation. One has just been married and the other has just lost a partner in a car crash. It is difficult to imagine how the same words could minister to both. But by inviting the congregation to place a stone in the baptismal water as an offering of our own prayers, and symbolising the immersion of our concerns in the love of God, both can engage with God in completely different ways. For one it becomes the exciting and joyful offering to God of a new relationship at the start of married life, a prayer for fruitfulness accompanied by a deep sense of joy. For the other it is about being surrounded by God and supported by all the other stones in the bowl at the time of deepest need, and is accompanied by tears.

Because of their multi-layered meaning, which can never be captured in words alone, symbols are singularly equipped to engage us with the indefatigable mystery of God in ways that word never can. Symbols themselves are symbols of the nature of God. The reality of God can never be expressed in words alone and can never be fully comprehensible to the human mind. Similarly symbols are always one step beyond explanation and therefore the most suitable vehicle of the God beyond words.

While symbols and action can be interpreted in different ways they also have a significance that goes beyond words. Even to talk of an 'interpretation' is to miss the point. We tend to ask the Enlightenment question, 'What is the meaning of a symbol?' and then expect an answer in words. Surely the point of symbol is that it goes beyond words and resonates with something deep within our humanity. The depth of love communicated by a kiss can never be expressed adequately in words. That is why we kiss. To ask what a kiss means is a facile question. Only the kiss itself communicates the meaning.

Symbolic untruth – a spiritual health warning

Beware! Our use of symbol will inevitably convey unintended meanings. This uncontrollability is part and parcel of the nature of symbol and is what gives it its potential and its power. However, each person in a congregation will interpret a particular act through the filters of their own experience and understanding. Symbols evoke meanings that are unintended, but they may also evoke meanings that, from a Christian perspective, might be untrue, even heretical, or worse, dangerous.

There has to be a cautionary side to symbol. Its great value also becomes its great danger; that ultimately its meaning is beyond our control. This means that our worship can be much more open to the Holy Spirit who blows where he wills. It also means that it is open to other influences and interpretations of a less healthy nature. This is no argument for not using them but it is a warning to use them with care.

What gives symbols one meaning rather than another is the context in which they are used. For example, consider a candle. The candle can convey powerfully the truth that Jesus is a light in our darkness. But a candle also burns us whereas Jesus does not. Therefore the use of the candle should be used in such a way as to convey the intended truth rather than an unintended mistruth. One way to try to ensure that symbols convey the intended rather than the unintended message is to look at the context in which they are used.

Context gives meaning. Candles do not represent Jesus except where the context gives them that significance. But it is true that all context gives meaning and so we move into a theoretical interlude offered to us by Victor Turner.

Another theoretical interlude – fields of meaning

Victor Turner speaks of three different fields of meaning, each of which give us a different insight into the meaning of a ceremony or an action. The same can also be applied to text. The three fields are:

- positional fields
- operational fields
- exegetical fields.

The positional field

This focuses on what comes before and after. In other words we are looking at where a particular item comes in the context of the whole worship. Consider the Peace, for example. There are a number of places this could occur in a service. The two most popular are probably before the reception of communion in the Roman Catholic eucharistic rite and before the eucharistic prayer in most Anglican rites. Each has a different meaning dependent on where it takes place. If it is before the reception of communion as in the Roman Catholic rite, it signifies the need of the whole Body of Christ to be united before they receive communion. In the Anglican rite, though, it usually happens before the eucharistic prayer. This suggests a different model of priesthood. The whole Body needs to be reconciled before the eucharistic prayer begins because the whole Body is involved in the eucharistic celebration. A further dimension is offered by the possibility of sharing the Peace at the beginning of the service. This gives more a sense of welcome, or a ritual 'Hello'. The nuances change as the position changes. Hence this is the positional field.

The operational field

This is more concerned with who does what, who is the operator. A service that is led by one person only says something about the nature of leadership in that church. A service that uses only male leaders says something about the place of women in the community. A service that is completely adult-led says something about the place of children. By looking at who does what we can see how a community values its members and which ones it values the most. This is the operational field.

The exegetical field

This refers to the way an action or symbol is given meaning by an explanation or comment. It may be by the minister, by the reading of a passage of Scripture, or by some liturgical preliminary that creates a context of understanding for what is about to happen.

These three fields both create and limit the meaning of a symbol or action and, if we are aware of them, can help us to understand what is happening in the worship we are observing or sharing in.

By looking at where we do one thing in relation to another we can discover nuances to our worship that otherwise we might have never discovered. By looking at who does what our underlying beliefs about authority and community are revealed. By looking at what we say (usually too much) we can see how much we are opening up or closing down on the multiple meanings of worship.

The prison of churchmanship (ritualisation)

One of the difficulties with liturgical symbols, and I include sacraments here, is that many of them have been trapped in churchmanship conflicts for centuries. The use of symbols has been considered 'High Church'. One of the tasks of the Church today is to liberate these symbols from their churchmanship prison. After all, most of them are not 'Catholic', but biblical.

A newly ordained colleague once accompanied me to a local church for one of their special festivals. The church we were visiting was definitely 'Anglo-Catholic', and Steve was definitely not. The service was badly produced and conducted. We began with a procession. However, because the vestry was very close to the seats of the clergy we processed out of the vestry, past our seats to the back of the church, round the font, returning up the centre to the seats we had passed a few minutes earlier. After we had circumvented the font the inevitable happened. The front of the procession going back up the aisle hit the tail of the procession still coming down. As if that was not bad enough Steve, a rather bulky guy, got stuck between the font and the back wall, which did not help things. The service continued with this degree of underlying but unintended amusement. Steve was particularly struck by the incense. It was used at different points throughout the service, or to be more accurate, the thurible containing the incense was swung. For some reason the charcoal had failed to light so there was no sight of that wonderfully fragrant puff of smoke at any point, though we were treated to the frequent sight of two of the servers blowing with all their might on the charcoal. This seems to be symbolic of the Holy Spirit in the Church today – lots of wind but no real fire!

After the service we walked silently back to the car and Steve just asked, 'Can that be done well?' I suggested it could. He then said he would like to use incense when he first celebrated the Eucharist after he was ordained priest. This would be new to his almost exclusively Evangelical family and friends who were there, but we did it. In the service notes we explained that incense was used in the Temple and features in the Book of Revelation. The Bible mentions it almost a hundred times as integral both to the worship of the Old Testament and worship in heaven at the end of time. Only in a few cases is its use condemned, and that was when it was burned in honour of foreign gods. The implication is that it *should* be used in the worship of the one true God. We pointed out the different meanings to its symbolic use. This seemed to pacify most of those who were suspicious before the service, but the written notes were nothing compared to the experience that people had. Great clouds of incense filled the church as the whole congregation joined together in praise. As we sang 'Let our praise to you be as incense' we could visualise our praises rising to the throne of God. The use of incense took us beyond the words that tried to explain it and enabled people to engage with God in a new way. We had liberated one of those imprisoned symbols, at least for those who were present.

On another occasion, an international charismatic conference for about 550 people, we sang the same song with a huge bowl of incense in front of a large Bible. We moved from the song into singing in tongues as the incense filled the room. Afterwards, the minister of one of the largest and most noted Evangelical churches in England asked how he could use incense in the worship in his church.

Incense for its own sake is at worst dead ritual and at best pointless. However, when incense becomes a multi-sensory expression of our prayers rising to the heart of God we add a new dimension to our worship and encounter new depths in our worship. We are guilty of having locked up these wonderful symbols within the prisons of our theology, our churchmanship and our desire for control. These liturgical symbols need to be recovered for their effective use as channels for the free flow of God's grace within the whole Church.

The prison of tidiness (anaesthetisation)

One of the marks of our so-called modern world has been the anaesthetisation of society. Gradually people are protected from the pain and the power of life. Western society is distanced from the realities of life through our increasingly materialist society. Drink, drugs and the media have all conspired to distract us from and reduce our sensitivity to the world. When we have a headache we take an aspirin. This removes the effect of the headache but does nothing to deal with its cause. The pain is dealt with by us becoming anaesthetised to it.

In his book *Birdsong*, the author Sebastian Faulkes powerfully contrasts the horror of life in the trenches in the first world war with life back home on the streets of England. The folk back home did not want to know what was really happening to their soldiers and it was in the interests of the government to keep the population anaesthetised by propaganda. In *Birdsong* this distancing is taken to the point where communication between front-line soldiers and those who remained in England was impossible. At the end of the book the central character does not speak for ten years.

This is the nature of our society. After the disaster at the

Hillsborough football stadium in 1989 where 96 people were killed, police broke down because many of them had not seen dead bodies before. Death is now taken out of the family environment and is dealt with by funeral directors who 'undertake' to do all the nasty work for us. Drugs transport us from the drudgery of this life to another world. Computers take us out of reality altogether into a virtual reality of their own. Slowly, but with increasing speed, we are distancing ourselves from the messiness of life. The same is happening in the liturgical sphere.

I know of one situation where water had been thrown over the congregation as a sign of the promises that God gives to his people in baptism. For many it was a deeply prayerful moment. However, one woman was heard to comment, 'I am so glad I didn't get any on me because I have just had my hair done!'

Just look at the elements we use:

- water
- oil
- ash
- fire.[2]

By their nature they are messy. That is no accident. They are chosen (by God) to convey his uncontrollability, yet the way we tend to use them suggests a picture of a God who is about as wild as a cuddly toy.

Our desire for control has also led to us domesticating these elements. We use a spoonful of water at baptism; we put incense in a little pot with chains on; we use bread that neither looks nor tastes like bread; we use grape juice (or worse, blackcurrant juice) instead of wine; we use oil as if it is a controlled drug. Often we use these liturgical substances in such a way that we even negate their official meaning. Real baptism is an experience of death by drowning and then rising to new life with Christ. It is hard to imagine how you could drown someone with a spoon!

Symbols and sacraments are the wild, uncontainable vehicles of the wild, uncontainable grace of God. Their meaning is unleashed when we allow them to remind us of God's wildness. Our attempts to domesticate these symbols amounts to liturgical substance abuse. If they are to be of any real use in the Church's worship they need to be liberated from the straitjackets of churchmanship and domestication so that they can unlock the doors of our hearts to the Holy Spirit.

Engaging symbols

Even liberated symbolic worship gets us only halfway. The best of western Protestant worship presents the Gospel effectively in words, and more recently through multi-media. But words, by their nature, are of limited value. The best of western Catholic worship presents the Gospel effectively in ceremony and story, but the formalised ritual has too often limited the power of the symbols used. The problem is that while the Church may have developed expertise and experience in presenting the Gospel to people, we are not so good at enabling people to engage with the God behind the presentation.

All too often symbolic action happens 'up there'. People see it (or not), may interpret it for their own lives (or not), but rarely are people encouraged to engage with it personally. I believe that what was happening in those experiences of intercession mentioned earlier in the chapter was that people were not just listening to prayer, or having someone to offer their prayer for them, but they were personally engaging with the God to whom they were praying.

An example of this might be the ceremonies of Maundy Thursday. It has become the tradition in some parts of the Western Church to enact the story of Jesus washing the feet of his disciples at the Last Supper. This usually happens after the sermon that follows the gospel reading of the story. The presiding minister wraps a towel around their waist and washes the feet of volunteers from the congregation. It can be a moving experience to watch. The minister usually has some difficulty in getting the required number of volunteers, because no one wants to have their feet washed in public. One problem is that we dislocate the enacting from the telling of the story, but the real problem is that the enacted story is too 'up there'. It is distant. We present the story, but we have not found a way to enable people to engage with the experience. The volunteer members of the congregation have to struggle with the experience of foot-washing but to others it remains a presentation, no matter how good that presentation might be. Few people engage personally with it.

The Maundy Thursday example is symbolic worship, but what we really need is the anointing of our imagination to make it interactive, moving it from being a presentation of God's truth to an engagement with the God of truth. With this and other services, we need to find ways of enabling the whole worshipping congregation to engage with whatever is the enacted symbol, in this case the foot-washing.

Two approaches to growth

Each of these styles betrays a particular attitude to Christian formation. The presentational approach is rooted in an educational model of formation that values understanding and knowledge. It is a modernist, Enlightenment approach. The engagement approach has its roots in a relational model of formation that values relationship with, and experience of, God, and relates much more to our postmodern world.

The educational approach tends towards the idea that if we present the Christian Gospel to people they will think it through and either accept or reject it. It is concerned primarily with training and knowledge. The relational approach is less about presenting the Christian Gospel, and is more focused on engaging people with God. Rather than knowing *about* God the emphasis is on knowing God, and what people need to learn is mediated not through the medium of teaching, but of relationship. Hence it is by engaging the personhood of God that we grow.

Recent liturgical renewal

At the moment, many Christian Churches are going through a period of liturgical renewal. This is true of my own Church, the Church of England, which is getting used to *Common Worship*, a project that was launched in 2000 but which will continue for many years to come. Many other Churches are in the same situation; they are facing their second round of liturgical change in twenty years, leading to a lot of critical questioning. 'We had the Alternative Service Book in 1980! Why do we need another change now?' is the cry. This perspective sees the revision as just another lot of texts.

What has happened is more complicated than that. From the Anglican perspective the revisions of the 1970s and 1980s were about textual changes. They made the huge jump from sixteenth-century Cranmerian English into a modern idiom. The transition from so-called 'traditional' language to modern English was so massive that the impact on the Church was equally dramatic. The latest changes are more subtle in their impact, but behind them is a paradigmatic change that far exceeds the revisions of twenty years or more ago.

The current changes are not just textual, though textual changes are there because language itself has moved on over this period. We have begun to take seriously the challenge of inclusive language; we have recognised that sentences should be based around the dynamic nature of verbs rather than the static nature of nouns. We have realised that where we do use nouns it is better to move from conceptual to concrete idea; so the language in the 1980s texts is already dated.

Significant shifts

However, the major shifts have not been about text at all but the liturgy and worship of the Church has to come to terms with the shifting sands of our very culture. The challenge presented by liturgical revision at the moment is not so much how we change what we say, but how we change the way we 'do' worship. Behind the revisions lie a number of trends that are deeply embedded in the emerging culture. If we fail to address them in the way we plan and 'do' worship, the liturgy of the Western Church will spiral helplessly into irrelevancy.

These trends, which provide the background against which the current round of liturgical revision is taking place, underline the need to change the emphasis of what we do in worship:

- from the textual to the visual;
- from understanding to experience; and
- from presentation to engagement.

From Reformation/Enlightenment to postmodern

In effect, these three changes of emphasis are just manifestations of the culture shift from a Reformation/Enlightenment approach to life towards a more holistic life view. These trends in society and culture are bound to have an effect on our worship and the way we organise it. While the God we worship is unchangeable, the culture we live in is constantly evolving. If the worship of the Church is going to be in the cultural vernacular we need to be aware of, and take account of, the changes taking place around us. The alternative is to be members not of the Church but of the Preservation Society for Ancient Ritual.

From the textual to the visual

I have written about the way our culture has made this transition, yet the Church hangs on hopelessly to an outmoded medium of communication. Throughout the twentieth century the whole of our life has been invaded and changed, and we are now a visual rather than a verbal people.

From understanding to experience

The breakdown of confidence in the scientific worldview has been accompanied by a change of significance in the importance of mental engagement, or understanding. At one point in the 1980s it was thought that the scientific, mathematical and philosophical basis of knowledge would soon be discovered, as mathematicians and physicists searched for the Unified Theory of Everything. This tantalising theory, which as the title suggests would provide a basis for explaining everything, has proved more elusive than expected. What has become obvious instead is that the more we know, the more we realise we do not know. The significance of understanding, or confidence in our ability to understand, has dwindled. Over the past twenty years people have realised that the scientific project is not going to produce the long-awaited goods. We have rediscovered the multi-dimensionality of our human nature, and the experiential and the relational have taken over from comprehension and fact as the ways we relate to the world. In the same way, we need to organise and plan our worship with the aim of enabling worshippers primarily to experience God rather than understand theology.

From presentation to engagement

Another consequence is that our liturgy should no longer try simply to present the truth of the Gospel, whether through preaching or drama, ceremony or ritual. Instead we need to find ways to draw the congregation into an engagement with God. People are no longer satisfied with a good explanation, but need to experience for themselves the truth of the Gospel. This key movement is one from presentation to engagement, and I shall be exploring it further in the next chapter.

Symbols transcend words and allow us to speak beyond the limitations of language. They enhance our possibilities of communication. While the use of the language of symbol opens up new opportunities in worship there is still further we need to travel. Moving from a word to a symbolic presentation of the Gospel is one thing, but the more significant step is the next one, moving from presentation to engagement.

Summary

Throughout this book I have repeated the point that we live in a world where words fail us. We therefore need to find a new, or recover a lost, means of communicating our love and praise of God. In moving beyond words we enter into the realm of symbol and action. Because they are open to multiple interpretations (polyvalence) they provide a situation where the whole congregation can share the same environment (seeing the same symbol or performing the same action) yet each person interprets this in their own personal way. Finally, I suggested three key movements, or shifts, that have been taking place in worship over the past few years.

Chapter 7
Engaging Worship

For preachers and worship leaders few experiences are more confidence-sapping than standing in front of a congregation facing a blank stare of apathetic resistance. For over a year I had encouraged the congregation to respond in positive ways to the challenge of the Gospel, but I felt I was getting nowhere. The church had many strong points, but making an overt demonstration of its faith was not one of them. Faith was there, but getting people to show it publicly was a different matter. I had tried to encourage people to share their stories with one another, but failed; encouraged them to tell one another the good things God was doing, but failed. All I saw were those deathly, blank stares and a lot of unresponsive people pinned to their pews.

However, on the day when we remember the baptism of Jesus, I tried something out of the ordinary for us. The 'custom' at this celebration had been to bless the water in the font and then to sprinkle (or in my case actually throw) water over the congregation as a reminder of the promises God makes to us in baptism. This time, though, I felt an inner compulsion to do something different. Instead of doing a solo procession around the church to an anthem, dousing anything that moved (and also things that did not, to the great annoyance of the people on the sound desk), I invited the congregation to come out of the pews that seemed to have such a hold on their posteriors and approach the font. I told them that they could make the sign of the cross on their own forehead as a sign of their commitment to Christ and offer whatever prayer they wanted as they did it. I issued the invitation, dipped my hand in the water and made the sign of the cross on my forehead so that everyone could see exactly what was expected. Then I looked. To my horror no one was moving. I was on my own, isolated, defeated by the pew glue. Then sud-

denly, and almost en masse, the congregation moved. There were a few who remained in their seats but I would estimate that 85–90 per cent of the congregation came to the font. I was amazed and overcome with tears.

Later, a colleague asked someone why people had responded as they did on that particular occasion rather than any other. The answer was, 'He gave us permission to do what we wanted to do rather than telling us to do what he wanted us to.'

Missionary culture

Towards the end of the last chapter I suggested that three major shifts were needed to make our worship relate more to the changing society around us:

- from the textual to the visual;
- from understanding to experience;
- from presentation to engagement.

All three are significant, but the *most* significant is the move from presentation to engagement.

For centuries the Western Church, wearing its missionary clothes, has been obsessed with presenting the Gospel of Christ to the world in every way it thought possible. There is nothing wrong with taking the Great Commission seriously. Laying the love of God before the world is at the heart of being Christian whether it is done through evangelism, social action or worship. Increasingly, though, it is recognised that words are not necessarily the best method. This is not a new piece of theology. Nine hundred years ago St Francis told his brothers to 'Go and preach the gospel and use words if necessary'. It might not be new theology but only as the old certainties of modernism have begun to break down have we begun to realise that laying the love of God before the world is more than an intellectual exercise.

Worship has its place in this. St Paul had a vision of God where the Truth would be encountered not as a clever argument, but in the worship of the Church.

If, therefore, the whole church comes together and all

> speak in tongues, and outsiders or unbelievers enter, will they not say that you are out of your mind? But if all prophesy, an unbeliever or outsider who enters is reproved by all and called to account by all. After the secrets of the unbeliever's heart are disclosed, that person will bow down before God and worship him, declaring, 'God is really among you.' (1 Corinthians 14:23–5)

Paul seems to think that even the non-believer should come to church and encounter God. In this context it is through the gift of prophecy but I see nothing in the text, or in my experience, to suggest that such an encounter can only happen through the exercise of a particular spiritual gift. John Wesley had a similar kind of understanding and expectation of worship when he referred to the communion service as a 'converting ordinance'. Worship, according to St Paul and John Wesley, should lead us to a life-changing engagement with God.

St Paul and John Wesley are not alone in presenting these expectations to the Church. As I pointed out in a previous chapter, relationship is the foundation of a truly biblical theology of worship, but our western Enlightenment mentality and English reserve has undermined this.

While this may have been the expectation of St Paul and John Wesley, it has not been the expectation of the Western Church at least for the past few hundred years. Rather than engage with God, we have found as many mechanisms as possible to keep him at arm's length. I once invited a well-known preacher to our church for a day. He looked at the Evensong (Book of Common Prayer) congregation, stood quietly in the pulpit and began his sermon: 'Do you know why people always sit at the back at Evensong?' *Pause.* 'So that if God really does turn up they can be the first out of the door!'

Preaching for a response

I would not want to suggest that engagement has been completely absent from our worship 'tool kit'. It has put its head above the parapet from time to time, but usually within the context of a sermon. Evangelicals often speak of 'preaching for a response', and I want to commend this. The classic form is the 'appeal', where the preacher will invite people to respond to the sermon by coming to the front for some public declaration of conversion or recommitment. This is an attempt to engage people with the God who has been preached. The problem is that it puts people in an awkward situation. We want them to respond in our way rather than their own, loading onto them our expectations of what a true response to God ought to be, rather than letting them find their own appropriate response.

It seems to me that too often, with the best of intentions, we create an uncomfortable, perhaps dangerous, environment and then ask people to respond. It is likely that even those who do respond will only allow God to do relatively safe things because the whole situation can make them feel so insecure. Surely we need to create a safe environment for God to do dangerous things rather than create a dangerous environment where people only allow God to do safe things? It only takes a little imagination to do this, but it usually means the worship leader having to hand control of each response over to God. For many of us this is just too risky. Jesus warned about the lawyers placing burdens on the people of his day: 'Jesus said, "Woe also to you lawyers! For you load people with burdens hard to bear, and you yourselves do not lift a finger to ease them" ' (Luke 11:46). Do they not apply just as much to the burdens we place on people and the obstacles we place before people who really do want to respond to and engage with God?

A little imagination can transform the situation. A story I recently heard is of Bill Hybels, the leader of the Willow Creek Community. In his presentation of the Gospel (a sermon using all the technology available) he told how one of his professors at university had preached. At the end of the professor's sermon he invited any of the students who wanted to take a next step in their lives to go and visit him. Bill went. There was an empty chair in the room. The professor suggested that Bill just talk to the empty chair as if Jesus was sitting there. He admitted that he felt self-conscious, but summoned up the courage to do it and it proved to be a significant moment for him in his life of faith. But it demands a certain kind of person to be able to cope with that kind of response. Bill then concluded his sermon with a period of quiet reflection where he invited all the people there to talk 'in their mind' to Jesus, as if they were talking face to face. They didn't have to speak out loud. Quiet music was played, which created a sense of personal space in the auditorium, and all the external negative pressures were removed. He gave space for every person to respond, and allowed everyone the opportunity to say what they wanted. But he had to lose control of the response and leave that to the individual and to God.

This is an example of how a response to a sermon can lead us from presentation to engagement. I would dare to suggest that all sermons should have a parallel ending to this, so that we are invited to move from presentation to engagement; from understanding to experience. It only takes a little imagination – and a willingness to 'let go' on the part of the preacher!

Worshipping for a response

While Evangelicals and charismatics have for centuries been preaching for a response, they have rarely been able to make the leap of imagination to see that worship can also be organised and led 'for a response'. I believe that spoken word and enacted symbol should dovetail into each other, reinforce each other and encourage each other. They should each form a different aspect of one seamless dynamic flow through an act of worship. It is possible to worship for a response as well as preach for a response.

Keeping God at bay

The Church has developed all sorts of clever ways to avoid engagement. One is style. While I was on sabbatical I realised just how manipulative Anglican worship is. I am accustomed to facing criticisms about charismatic worship being manipulative, how it 'whips up' the emotions, puts social pressure on people to be 'ministered to' and how leaders can abuse their power and make people feel guilty if they do not react in a certain way. I am convinced that in England, at least, this is not such a great problem, as charismatics, more than any others, are aware of the dangers that inhabit their territory and take steps to avoid it.

But this is not a claim often lodged against mainstream western Christian worship.

What became obvious to me while I was in America was just how controlling Anglican, and indeed most western worship, is. Rather than encouraging a particular style of response from the worshipping congregation the Anglican 'style' tries to suppress response. The whole culture creates an expectation, and consequent pressure, to conform to orderliness. This makes any response from individuals within the body difficult, and therefore unlikely. The president tightly controls the whole thing. The way the services are led allows little time or space for the spontaneous to break in. While it may be tasteful and ordered, the whole context is just as manipulative as any charismatic meeting; it is just that the purpose of the manipulation is different. The purpose is to keep God at arm's length but to disguise it as dignity. While my criticisms here are aimed at Anglicans, I would encourage all worship leaders to look at the way that services are organised and led. How repressive and controlling a culture or style do we create?

The relative clause

In this book so far I have avoided textual issues, but they arise here. The Liturgy of the Anglican Church, and indeed of most liturgical Churches, is riddled with prayers about God that keep God at a distance. We speak *about* him, but rarely *to* him. One of the classic techniques used here is the relative clause – the use of the word 'who'. For example, in prayers we often find phrases like:

> *Almighty God,*
> who *sent your Son Jesus Christ to be our Saviour* . . .

I have always found phrases like this problematic. They irritate me. Since the use of the relative clause in this way is an outmoded speech pattern, it doesn't seem suitable for use in contemporary worship. No one would speak to me and say, 'Peter, who has travelled from the far distant town of Leeds . . .'. We just do not speak like that. One of the principles of the liturgical Reformation was that worship should be offered in the vernacular, the language of the day. This is not the language of today.

Relative clauses can also create a different problem altogether, in that the relative clause creates a prayer which keeps God at a distance. We continue the address in the third person and fail to address God directly. We do not engage with him, but linguistically keep him at arm's length. This may seem almost insignificant, but relationships are largely conducted within the context of a language and if the language keeps the principal subjects at arm's length, the result will be relationship conducted at arm's length. God will for ever remain distant.

Now look at the normal mode of address:

> *Almighty God,*
> you *sent your Son Jesus Christ to be our Saviour . . .*

Here we are addressing God directly and the use of 'you' draws us into an engagement with God. There is no longer an arm's length relationship, but a closer one and this kind of language will have an influence on the way our relationship develops. These relative clauses could easily be purged from our liturgical tool kit, so why keep them? The answer, I fear, is that they serve our unconscious purposes of keeping a dangerous God at a safe distance.

Too much of our liturgy speaks *about* God rather than *to* God. I suggest that most of our worship texts need to make this shift from presentation to engagement. Text is not the whole of liturgy, but it is a part of it, and we ignore it at our peril. I am glad to say that some of these textual changes are already happening. In my own Church's liturgical reform we have a good example of this in the change of responses used before and after the reading of the gospel at a communion service. They used to be acclamations about God, speaking about him and treating God in the third person:

Before the gospel is read

Reader   A reading from the Gospel according to Matthew
             (*for example*).

All   **Glory to Christ our Saviour.**

After the gospel has been read

Reader   This is the Gospel of Christ.
All   **Praise to Christ our Lord.**

Now the responses have been changed from comments about God to direct praise of God. We address God personally.

Before the gospel is read

Reader   Hear the Gospel of our Lord Jesus Christ according to Matthew (*for example*).
All   **Glory to *you*, O Lord.**

After the gospel has been read

Reader   This is the Gospel of the Lord.
All   **Praise to *you*, O Christ.**

The textual change moves into an engagement with the God we meet in the reading of the Scripture. This in itself is not going to change the world, but if we employ the same criteria throughout our liturgy we will create a more relational environment through which people can encounter and engage with God.

Traditional language

The same can be said of the use of 'traditional' language, whether it be sixteenth-century English or Latin. The use of traditional language has the effect of formalising and restricting the speech code. It may produce an elegant, even beautiful text, but the impact it has on the relational dynamic between worshipped and worshipper is undesirable.

The use of Latin, particularly where a congregation does not understand the language, creates an even greater relational gap. It establishes a hierarchy where the priests, who understand the language, celebrate on behalf of the laity who do not. The priests are the only ones who can really speak to God. The impact on the relationship is that God is pushed further and further beyond the horizon of our life. Engagement becomes extremely unlikely and so relationship impossible.

Tongues

Some would suggest that we could make the same criticisms of the use of tongues in worship. Here we praise God (or intercede or confess) in a language that we do not understand. So should tongues be discouraged? No, and to suggest otherwise is to completely misunderstand both the dynamics and purpose of the gift of tongues.[1] While the mind may not understand what the mouth is saying when a person prays in tongues, the heart 'knows' a depth of praise that far exceeds human words. The heart is drawn deeper into a relationship with God because words do not become an obstacle. We can all relate to the situation where a lover tells the beloved, 'I love you more than words can say.' In tongues, God the Beloved gives us the lovers those words. Our hearts understand them even if our minds do not. In this way tongues bypass the mind and lead us to a profound encounter of love with God.

The gift of tongues has appeared again and again throughout the history of the Church. I cannot help but wonder if its appearance in the twentieth century is one of the first signs of the breakdown of modernism. It emerged on the scene when we lived in a word-based culture. We had a profound cultural need to express our love for God verbally. So God gives the gift that uses words, but bypasses the mind to draw us into a deeper encounter with him. It is a postmodern phenomenon in modernist clothes.

A deeper reality

However, the whole thrust has to be more than just words. Text is at most 10 per cent of liturgy. I was recently speaking to a friend who is the minister of a charismatic Baptist church about how worship, particularly praise, enabled people to express their relationship with God. I suggested that what might be happening is that only the extroverts were really 'going with it' and the introverts, rather than being part of it, might actually feel marginalised, maybe even guilty that they could not enter into the spirit of praise that others were enjoying. To my surprise he agreed and we discussed the question of how the introverted personality engages with God.

The use of interactive, symbolic action or gesture, can engage people of all kinds of personality types. We have to go beyond words because they limit our possibilities. The great philosopher of language, Ludwig Wittgenstein, spent his latter years looking at the mystery of language and its limitations. We are only just beginning to realise the significance of his work for worship as our deepening understanding of the mystery of our humanity bring us right up against the limitations of language – not just our language, but language itself.

The Eucharist

This thrusts us into the world of symbol, a world that Jesus was more than happy to inhabit. Take, for example, the Eucharist. It is the ultimate example of moving from presentation to engagement. First, Jesus takes bread and wine and uses them as symbols of his life and purpose.

'This is my body, given for you.'
'This is my blood, shed for you and for many for the forgiveness of sins.'

At this point he has related bread and wine to himself. There is a real symbolic relationship, so that from now on bread and wine will always have a deeper significance to the disciples. But Jesus moves from presentation to engagement as he invites the disciples to eat the bread and drink the wine. It is not enough to remain distant. We not only have to move close and engage, but we have to take those signs of his life and purpose into ourselves. This is the ultimate in parabolic worship.

I am fascinated that for centuries sacramental theologians have fought over the theology of the Eucharist. Churches have even put people to death because of their disputes. But Jesus did not give us text or theology. He gave us action; something to do in remembrance of him. He gave us bread and wine, not a theological treatise. It is a serious question to ask whether this giving of symbols was intentional. So much of the Church's energy has been spent on the futile and unintended quest of trying to establish one explanation over another. Why can theologians not see that Jesus gave us symbols rather than words because symbols push us beyond the limits of language's capability? By definition there will always be polyvalence about symbol, and particularly the Eucharist.

This action is itself symbol and as such can never be captured by words alone. Symbol defies our linguistic prison. That is its nature. And it takes us beyond the basic elements of bread and wine into the mystery of the love of God that is at its heart. That is what Jesus gave us, and intended to give us: elements – action – symbol. Who are we to assume that he wanted us to have more? It is ironic that while Jesus gave us action we have constructed cities of theological libraries in our insecurity and our need to draw precise meaning from what is, at its heart intentionally imprecise. The Eucharist is for me the clearest example that liturgy is at best 10 per cent text and that we should concentrate not so much on what we say as what we do.

We also see in the Eucharist the paradigm of parabolic worship, where the movement from presentation to engagement is complete – where the symbolic action is clear but we are not left as mere spectators. Instead we are drawn into the reality of the symbol to experience the life it represents, i.e. makes present again.

Educational parallels

In a way, what I have suggested is not far removed from some of the developments that have become normal in the world of education. For a few decades now the emphasis has moved inexorably from the one teacher standing at the front imparting knowledge to a class to a more interactive style of learning through which people learn as much through experience as through the impartation of knowledge.

Nowadays so much learning is done through experience. In fact, many educational theorists would doubt that there is any other type of learning. Parabolic worship, with this move from presentation to engagement, is a similar development in worship.

In the last chapter I made a comment about how the Church deskills so many lay people with the consequence that they remain silent in our churches. If we can make this shift from presentation to engagement and allow the members of our worshipping congregations to take control of their own response to God, then I believe this will affirm them and will eventually encourage them to take greater responsibility for all aspects of the Church's life.

The Principle of Reciprocity

The Cherokee tell a story.

> There is a gorge in Cherokee country, which used to be a sacred toll path. The Little People lived there. If a Cherokee wanted to walk along the path that ran through the gorge they had to pay a toll. The toll was to place a small pebble on a pile of pebbles at the entrance to the gorge. One day, a young brave tried to be clever and test whether the Little People really did guard the path. He didn't put a stone on the pile but just walked on. He walked a few paces when he felt a stone hit his ankle. It had come from nowhere. He walked a few more paces. Another stone hit him on his hip but this time it was a bigger stone. He walked a few paces more and this time a very large stone hit him on the chest. He stopped out of fear for his life, went back, placed a pebble on the pile, then walked through unhindered.

There are many stories like this in Cherokee mythology and they all share a common feature. Whenever you take something, put something back! It is called the Principle of Reciprocity and it is applied to every aspect of Cherokee life.

Nowadays the Cherokee live like any other Americans. Although there was a time when they hunted to survive, they never went out to pillage the land. There were various rituals that they employed in the hunting process. In the diary of my time with the Cherokee I recorded this conversation with one of the local leaders.

> He explained how the Cherokee do not take life lightly. When they go hunting they do not kill the first animal they see, no matter how hungry they are, nor do they kill the second. They always wait until they see the third before they kill. Before they kill they pray, asking permission from the animal to kill it. And when they kill an animal they ask forgiveness of God and the animal for having killed it. They then make an offering and leave something where they have killed the animal. This is the Principle of Reciprocity. They do not take life without putting something back. He did not say what this might be and I did not want to interrupt him. The questions seemed less important than listening at the time.

So much of Cherokee life and ritual is focused on this wise principle. Its simplicity heaps profound criticism on our materialistic, consumer society where we think that money is the answer to everything, where we do not just take, but take to the point of extinction.

I believe that the Principle of Reciprocity has significant implications for worship, especially if we want to move the emphasis from presentation to engagement. Our worship ought to be a paradigm of this principle. St Paul wrote:

> I appeal to you therefore, brothers and sisters, by the mercies of God, to present your bodies as a living sacrifice, holy and acceptable to God, which is your spiritual worship. Do not be conformed to this world, but be transformed by the renewing of your minds, so that you may discern what is the will of God – what is good and acceptable and perfect. (Romans 12:1–2)

It is the presenting of ourselves as a living sacrifice that *is* our worship. Yet our worship is also a response. As the Letter of John reminds us: 'We love because he [God] first loved us' (1 John 4:19). But the writer goes further: 'In this is love, not that we loved God but that he loved us and sent his Son to be the atoning sacrifice for our sins' (1 John 4:10). The process has a compelling simplicity: God loves us so much he gave us Jesus; we return God's love by offering ourselves.

This *is* worship. Without the operation of this principle there might be the performance of a liturgy, there might be the presentation of ritual and ceremony, but there is no real worship, at least not in any Christian sense.

Here we see why a presentational approach can never take us to the heart of real worship. It is one-way worship and only enacts the first part of the dynamic. As we move from presentation to engagement we do so through the process of offering. As we offer ourselves to God we are caught up in that divine dynamic of worship through which we are transformed into the people God wants us to be.

- We offer ourselves to God.
- God takes that offering.
- God transforms it into the likeness of Jesus.
- God gives it back to us transformed.

A friend of mine talks about 'Ahh moments'. They are those times in worship when we are so touched by the presence of God that all we can say is 'Ahh!' I am convinced that those significant 'Ahh moments' are tied up with this Principle of Reciprocity. They are the times when for one reason or another we are able to offer at least part of ourselves to God through some aspect of the worship. When we receive that part back, transformed, it has an experiential effect on us. In simple words, we *feel* the transformation. We have entered into the process of worship through which the people of God are transformed. Where we do not see the people of God being radically transformed, could that be because there is little or no real offering taking place in what are supposed to be our 'services'?

By extrapolation it is also possible to see how the Principle of Reciprocity at the heart of worship could have an impact on our world. If we always put something back when we took something we would not be desperately searching for alternatives to the resources we have used up, we would not be searching for ways to stop our earth overheating, and we would not be spiralling towards our own mass suicide. It seems clear to me that the Principle of Reciprocity leads to the sustaining and transformation of creation.

Applying the Principle of Reciprocity

Most forms of worship, liturgical and so-called non-liturgical, have clear opportunities to apply this kind of responsive offering.

- *The Opening* of our worship is, (or ought to be) the laying before God of our lives as they are. Whatever way we begin our service, the introductory rite is about our coming into the presence of God, or God coming into our midst, so that we can be transformed by the offering of lives.
- *The Confession* is about offering to God our sinfulness and its working out in our lives and the lives of others. We give it to God so that he might take it from us, cleanse us with his love, and – dare we ask – undo some of the effects of our sin.
- *Hearing the Word of God* is about offering ourselves to God so that his word takes root in our open hearts.
- *The financial Offering* is a symbol of the offering of our lives.
- *The eucharistic Offering* is not just bread and wine, but ourselves so that they, and we, might be transformed into the Body of Christ.

Part of the problem is that we have lost our understanding of this dynamic. Our cultural journey over the past five centuries has led us on a different path. Worship that takes this principle seriously is risky, because it not only presents us with the opportunity for transformation but brings with it a threat to our comfortable, consumer lifestyle.

The Principle of Reciprocity is the centre of worship that leads us to engagement with God. It need not, however, be a great ordeal. There is an assumption that a response to God must be overtly demonstrative. This is a myth created by extroverts or ministers who need to know what is going on in their congregations for their own security or reputation. The response of individuals to God will vary as much as people's lives vary. The aim is to create those opportunities for everyone to respond in a way that is right for them individually. In many cases this is not so much about doing new things in worship but about drawing out the inner meaning of elements that are already there. It is about providing safe ways for people to engage with a dangerous God.

TWO EXAMPLES

In order to explore the difference this shift from presentation to engagement might have on the way we prepare for worship I want to explore the impact it could have on two particular services: funerals and marriages. While local traditions proliferate in both of these there are also strong common themes that transcend tradition. More importantly, they are services that sit on the boundary between Church and society. They are based on human, not just Christian, events. Death happens to everyone, and marriage has always been considered a 'gift of God in creation'.[2] In other words, it is a way God touches everyone with his grace regardless of their theological persuasion. This is why most Churches have always been prepared to conduct the marriage of non-Christians. Because of this, wedding and funeral services provide the Church with special opportunities for evangelism through worship. They are services that particularly need to take account of the changing patterns, assumptions and expectations of our surrounding culture so that we speak through these acts of worship in a language that can be understood by those participating in them.

So let us look at how the services around death and marriage might be shaped by attempts to make them more visual, experiential and engaging.

The funeral service

I have always maintained that funerals are relatively easy because people come to them ready to reflect on the deep questions of life. In order to do a funeral badly you really have to do something awful, like use the wrong name. The challenge of a funeral is not to give people 'off-the-peg' answers, but to enable them to engage with the God of life and death who can give them light in their darkness and hope in their despair. Traditionally we have used the opportunity for a sermon to do this, but more and more we are realising that what we do, as well as what we say, at funerals can have a significant impact.

From the textual to the visual

The most powerful visual element is a 'given' – the presence of the body or a coffin. This represents so much for the mourners: the relationships they had with the deceased; the memories they carry; the experiences they shared. But often its presence is treated as an embarrassment rather than as a focus. As the main visual focus it is important that the coffin can be seen. This may seem to be stating the obvious, but in a society distanced from death there may be a temptation to keep the pain represented by the body or the coffin as far away as possible.

At the funeral service we speak a lot about Jesus' victory over death in the resurrection. This can be visually presented by the lighting of a large (the Easter) candle,[3] expressing the victory of our Lord Jesus Christ over death. The lighting of the candle could be accompanied by something like:

Leader   We light this candle to remind us that when our
           Lord Jesus Christ was raised from the dead he
           defeated the powers of darkness and death.

The candle is then lit.

**All   Lord, by your cross and resurrection you have set
           us free. You are the Saviour of the world.**

At the committal the coffin could be touched or a hand laid upon it by the minister or members of the family. This would suggest to the family that God can touch the deceased, even in death.

When most clergy or worship leaders plan a service, they begin with the text and then (maybe) go on to ask how we can illustrate the text with some action, ceremony, ritual or dramatic representation. I believe we need to change our mode of thinking so that the first consideration is the core message we want to convey. Then, what can we do to present this? Only finally should we consider what words are appropriate. The priority should be visual over textual.

From understanding to experience

There are a number of emotional reactions that we usually want to encourage among mourners, particularly the family. Our hope is that they will go away having experienced something of the comforting presence and touch of God in and through the service. We also hope that they will be able to face their own feelings about the death of their loved one. We can encourage this verbally. However, actions speak louder than words. The new *Common Worship* funeral service of the Church of England offers the opportunity for the chief mourners to place objects of significance on the coffin. If carefully chosen, such actions allow them not only to engage with the liturgy (see the next point) but it also enables them actively to express something of their deepest emotions. Silence can create an opportunity for real grief to emerge. It can also create the environment for God's Holy Spirit to meet with the family and be their Comforter. But we need to let the silence happen.

The effects of the distancing of the close family from death can also be reversed to some extent by them gathering around the coffin at an appropriate point in the service. This may be at the committal but the purpose would be to bring the deceased, and the pain of their death, close to the family.

From presentation to engagement

Over the past one hundred years the reality of death has been divorced more and more from the family experience. It is not that long since death happened at home and the women of the family 'laid out' the body; in some parts of the UK and possibly elsewhere this is still the practice. The deceased rested in the family home with the coffin lid off, and the men carried the coffin into church and filled in the grave. There was a lot of engagement with the reality of the death. Now, in western society, death is kept at a distance and people 'undertake' to deal with all the painful elements for us.

At the funeral we have an opportunity to re-engage with the reality of death. The use of silence can be effective here. People come bringing pain and we can provide space for them to engage with it. Tears are appropriate. As well as encouraging the family to place items on the coffin, or to touch the coffin as they leave the crematorium chapel, we could encourage everyone to throw soil or a flower in the grave. Many of the old traditional death rituals, now lost in so many communities, give us clues as how best to enable the family to relate to the reality of death.

We must not forget, though, that the primary engagement we are looking for is not so much with the reality of death, but with the God who is the Lord of life and death. One of the family members could light the Easter candle, or the family could be invited to light smaller candles from it and place them somewhere significant in relation to the coffin.

These are just a few ideas, but the ideas themselves are not particularly important. Ways forward will vary from place to place, and family to family. The important thing is that the right questions are asked about how we can be:

- more visual
- more experiential
- more engaging.

Marriage

We now move from a traumatic event to a celebratory one. Marriage congregations are often less interested in the service than the celebrations to follow. The 'churchy bit' is just an unnecessary preliminary so that nice photographs can be taken. Because of this, some ministers find weddings more difficult to conduct well than funerals. It is important to understand that the minister's task is different in these two services. Rather than having a service-ready group of people as you have at a funeral, the skill at a wedding is drawing reluctant people in.

From the textual to the visual

In western culture the marriage service already contains a lot of visual elements. There is the taking of hands, the giving of rings, the blessing of the couple. But most of this is hidden if the couple face away from the congregation. I once posed this problem to a group of clergy. One suggested that what we need to do is to sit the congregation in the chancel or sanctuary. I suggested that it might be a little easier if we just turned the couple round! Why not have the couple facing the congregation with the minister's back to the congregation as the couple are addressed? This would radically change the whole dynamic of the service. The congregation (and perhaps more importantly the video operator!) would see everything that happens.

The Anglican theology of marriage recognises the couple as ministers of their own sacrament, but a combination of the clericalisation of the Church, and the influence of the presentational model of worship, has caused the rite to be presented in such a way as to obscure this. To re-emphasise this, why not allow them to make their vows directly to each other rather than repeat them after the minister? The priestly role at this key point is taken from the minister and handed over to the real celebrants, the couple. This change was suggested by the rubrics of the then new service in *The Alternative Service Book 1980* but no one ever seemed to notice it! It continues in *Common Worship*, yet still the old practice goes on regardless of its origins in a time when the couples were usually illiterate and had to repeat the vows because they could not read them. With such levels of illiteracy a thing of the past, why do we continue with this?

Perhaps because of the Internet, and certainly because of the cross-fertilisation between Churches and cultures, many other kinds of ceremony are emerging on the scene. Some are helpful: others less so. Take, for example, the marriage candle. This is a special three-branched candlestick with two small candles and a large one in the middle. One way of using this candle is to light the two smaller ones and then, after the marriage, to light the larger one and extinguish the two smaller ones. I take issue with this, and would even dare to suggest that it is a symbolic form of heresy. Christians believe that the partnership of marriage is greater than the sum of the individual parts and therefore it is right to light the large candle, but the individuality of the two partners does not disappear, as is suggested by extinguishing the individual candles. I suggest that each partner lights their individual candle after they have declared their intention to marry the other. Then, after they have made their vows and exchanged rings, they both take a light from their individual candles and together light the large one, but leaving their individual candles lit. The minister could then announce that they are husband and wife.

For centuries in England the marriage registers were signed at the end of the service in the privacy of the vestry. I do not know why this practice developed but, as with all traditional ceremonies, there was probably a straightforward, practical reason. But why hide a feature of the service that might be of interest to everyone? Why not sign the registers straight after the couple are married so that everyone can see? Furthermore, by gathering the families around the registers the idea of marriage being not simply the coming together of two individuals, but of two families, is visually demonstrated.

Another ceremony gaining in popularity is that of the couple each drinking wine from a common cup after they are married. Wine is a biblical symbol of the Kingdom of God and so this is appropriate in a Christian marriage service. It may also 'connect' with the glass of wine (or whatever) offered to the guests at the reception.

There are many other ways of using symbolic action in the wedding service. I simply offer these to open up the subject and encourage you to ask what could be done in your church.

From understanding to experience

By placing a greater emphasis on the use of symbol in the wedding the couple can be more actively involved in the whole service, further reinforcing the idea that the couple are the ministers of the sacrament. It also enables the move from under-standing to experience to happen more naturally. By using different symbolic actions the couple begin their marriage by doing something together (lighting candles) and/or by sharing in something together (drinking from a common cup). The beginning of the marriage is no longer just words but involves them in shared action and experience.

From presentation to engagement

Who are we trying to 'engage' – the couple or the congregation? Of course, the answer is both, but we engage each in different ways. By conducting the wedding service in this kind of way, the couple are more clearly engaged as ministers of the sacrament.

This could be extended further by allowing the couple to participate in the general blessing of the congregation at the end of
the service.

However, engaging an often-unwilling congregation is a
different matter. The fact that there is more to see, and their
being more able to see it, can make a great deal of difference to
the congregation. The more there is to see (as opposed to hear)
makes any service more interesting to those reluctant to engage.

Summary

*From the practical perspective of planning worship three ques-
tions emerge from this chapter about how we can move the focus
of our worship from the textual to the symbolic or visual, from
understanding to experience, and from presentation to
engagement.*

*All three are important but the key is the third one, the move
from presentation to engagement. We need to be less concerned
with what the minister does, and more concerned with how the
whole worshipping body of Christ can participate in worship.
Worship was never meant to be a spectator sport. No minister
wants a large band of supporters. What is needed is a large team
of players, and in the context of today we need to ask God to
anoint our imaginations, so that worship planners and leaders
can create suitable opportunities for people to engage with God.*

*If we can begin to ask these kinds of questions about every
element within our services (entrance, greeting, confession, etc.),
worship will be transformed into an agent of God's creative power.
Let us dare to do this with every element of what we do, not
necessarily all at once but gradually and deeply, so that it is
not only our worship that is transformed, but ourselves.*

Chapter 8

Creating Worship

Picture the scene: a large conference for church leaders, primarily bishops and clergy from across the world. Most had travelled thousands of miles. Many had left behind churches whose futures were uncertain; some were unsure whether they might still be the bishop when they returned. The delegates carried huge burdens of responsibility.

The opening act of worship focused on Jesus going into the wilderness to be tested, but the conference organisers wanted that wilderness experience to be a positive rather than a negative one. Yet the tiredness and the pain had to be recognised. First, we used the story of Jesus going into the wilderness to do battle with the devil in Luke 4. Then followed a meditative reflection on the personal deserts that each had to walk in. The worship confronted people with the wilderness of their own lives.

Next, we used the canticle, The Song of the Wilderness:

**The ransomed of the Lord shall return
and sorrow and sighing shall flee away.**
The wilderness and the dry land shall rejoice: the desert shall blossom and burst into song. They shall see the glory of the Lord, the majesty of our God.
The ransomed of the Lord shall return with singing.
Strengthen the weary hands and make firm the feeble knees. Say to the anxious, 'Be strong, fear not, for your God is coming with judgement, coming with judgement to save you.'
The ransomed of the Lord shall return with singing.
Then shall the eyes of the blind be opened and the ears of the deaf unstopped.

Then shall the lame leap like a hart and the tongue of the
dumb sing for joy.
The ransomed of the Lord shall return with singing.
For waters shall break forth in the wilderness and streams in
the desert;
Joy and gladness shall be theirs, and sorrow and sighing shall
flee away.
The ransomed of the Lord shall return
and sorrow and sighing shall flee away.

(from Isaiah 35)

*Silence was kept for a short time, then, as the musicians led some
reflective worship, each person was invited to go to a bowl of dry
sand and hold the sand in their hands. As the sand slipped
through their hands they were invited to offer to God in prayer
their own wildernesses. As they moved away from the sand they
were unexpectedly given a flower to remind them that God will
make the desert blossom. In the eyes of many, tears were obvious.*

Defining terms

I was once helping to lead a post-ordination training conference
on creating worship. People were put into groups, each being
asked to prepare an act of worship for different parts of the
Church's year. The first one was looking at an Epiphany morning
prayer. They took one of the existing forms for this and simply
moved the items within it around. The flow from one item to
the next was strained to say the least. When asked why they had
produced this in their particular way they simply said that they
had been asked to be creative and they thought it meant that
they should move things around. Rather than being creative they
had actually destroyed the whole integrity of the service they
adopted. It was chaos, but all done in the name of creativity.

Something had clearly gone wrong with the initial teaching. At
the beginning of the conference we had (I thought!) made it clear
that designing creative worship was not primarily about changing the shape or the text of worship, doing clever things with
candles or rock, or hugging trees while chanting new versions

of Psalm 150. It is rather about using every means possible to create the right environment for a formative encounter with God.

The value of our worship is not founded on its beauty, professionalism, dignity, cleverness, educative value, musical quality, or anything else. The real value of worship is dependent on whether or not it enables a formative encounter between God and us, whether it leads to true engagement.

I have already given a definition of *encounter* as a formative engagement with God that makes us more the people God intends us to become. Creative worship happens when we make opportunities for a formative engagement with God.

But first, why do we need to do this? Over the past twenty or so years the Church's confidence in its life and purpose has dwindled away, and this has shown itself in worship. There have been a number of strategic retreats of the 'going backwards' rather than the 'time for prayer' variety.

The first method of retreat is *fossilisation*. This is where a ceremony, or a particular way of performing the ceremony, becomes more important than the reason for doing it. Some sociologists of religion might argue that all ritual falls into this category. In fossilisation, aspects of our worship become obscure and no longer relate to the root purpose. Often this goes hand in hand with an assumption that if people do not encounter God it is their own fault, rather than that of the way the liturgy is celebrated. Prissiness becomes more important than power.

*Without the mice, Nesbit's role
became purely ceremonial.*

Another method of retreat is *rejectionism*. Here the blame is put totally at the door of the way we worship, and this is perhaps most clearly expressed by many charismatics and Reformation-minded Protestants who suggest that liturgy itself impedes the free-flowing of the Spirit. Consequently, attempts are made to 'liven up' the liturgy or it is rejected altogether in favour of what is thought to be freedom.

Miss Jones tried to enliven the Litany with a Mexican wave.

Both of these extremes are gaining ground in our churches today, but both betray a basic misunderstanding of liturgy and worship. We do not need to retreat into ritualism nor do we need to reject the patterns of worship that have moulded Christians for centuries. The real task of the creative liturgist, or worship planner, is to rediscover the inner dynamic and power of liturgical worship and learn again how to unlock it.

Enacted parable

The Old Testament offers many examples of the way in which the force of a prophecy or truth was elaborated by acting it out. These enacted symbols, or acted parables, communicated the truth of a message far more powerfully than words ever could, and demonstrate once again that words are limited in their value in teaching as well as in worship.

The Old Testament is rife with examples. When an Israelite slave wanted to offer himself into permanent slavery rather than live in the freedom that was his by right, the owner would pierce his ear, fastening him to the doorpost to declare that the slave was now a permanent part of the household (Exodus 21:6). Shoes were given to declare the surrender of all rights of inheritance (Ruth 4:7). Circumcision demonstrated the entrance of the child into the life of the community. A scapegoat was released on the Day of Atonement and the sins of the people were transferred onto it (Leviticus 16). Another similar example records the passing of uncleanness onto a red heifer (Numbers 19).

The prophets were also astute in this kind of activity. Enacted parable (or prophecy) was used not only to proclaim a message but also to demonstrate what God might do. So, Isaiah went naked to show that God would bring poverty and political exile to Israel (Isaiah 20:2). Jeremiah buried a new linen loincloth and later dug up the ruined girdle to show how Israel had been rejected (Jeremiah 13). Ezekiel drew out a city on a tile and made siege-engines to surround it to foretell the future destruction of Jerusalem (Ezekiel 4:1–3).

Jesus himself used enacted parable to convey truths beyond words. The driving out of the money-changers from the Temple (Matthew 21:12f), the miracles of the loaves and the fishes (John 6:1f) and the walking on water (Matthew 14:22f) are all enacted parables that speak far more powerfully than words. The ultimate enacted parable of course, which moves people beyond words and can never be fully explained, is the cross itself.

The enacted parable or prophecy has an established history in Scripture. By using this tool the protagonists drew their hearers and watchers into the reality they were trying to communicate. They moved from presentation to engagement.

Enacted Scripture

I want to suggest that we employ a similar approach to Scripture in our worship today and that one effective way of moving from a presentational approach to an engaging one is to encourage people to enter into and experience the truths to which Scripture alludes. I am not saying that the sermon does not have its place but Scripture itself, as we have seen, goes beyond the use of words. This kind of liturgical biblicism can take us beyond a purely mental appreciation into an experience of truth that deeply affects our humanity. I gave an example of this at the beginning of this chapter, showing the application of one passage, but there are many in Scripture that lend themselves to liturgical adaptation. This already happens a number of times in the Christian year:

- placing the kings, or the gifts, in the crib at Epiphany and relating them to our lives;
- using water at the celebration of the baptism of Jesus;
- lighting candles at Candlemas (the Feast of the Presentation of Christ);
- making the sign of the cross in ash on the worshippers' foreheads on Ash Wednesday;

and so on.

These examples form part of the liturgical tool kit of many western churches and they present us with some of the most evocative worship of the year. I suggest that we could 'enact' Scripture much more than we do. If, as happened in the example at the beginning of the chapter, we hear about God making the desert blossom, why not have something of the desert and something of the blossoming? If Scripture speaks of God quenching our thirst, why not drink? If Scripture speaks of turning our hearts of stone to hearts of flesh why not touch stones or our hands and faces? If Scripture talks about God being the Lord of all time, why not do something with our diaries?

Of course, we need to avoid gimmickry. The purpose of this approach is to create the environment for a formative encounter with God, not to distract people by making them cringe. The Church is good enough at that already. Scripture is alive with vibrant images that can have a direct impact on the way we worship. Let's use them.

The creative process: one approach

Practically, though, how do we do this? Here is one possible way through the process.

- Choose the Bible passage you are going to use.
- Look for the images, symbols or actions. Do not be afraid of the obvious. Let the Bible do as much work for you as possible.
- Ask how those images resonate with the life of your congregation. What points of contact are there? Do not be afraid to be specific; the greater the range of interpretation you use the greater will be the relevance, and consequently the take-up.
- Decide on the main point that you hope to make. How do you want people to end up – emotionally/physically? What do you hope they will experience?
- Be aware of what resources (objects and people) are needed to enable the process to happen.
- See how you can make this fit seamlessly into the service. Might it fulfil the function of an existing part of the service, e.g. the confession, the intercessions? What should precede and follow the action?
- Find ways to help people to engage without making them feel too self-conscious. Could music, subdued or selective lighting, or the location help?
- Make sure you have everything necessary to enable things to proceed smoothly and without causing distress to those participating. Walk through it, mentally at least, but preferably physically. That way you are more likely to see the problems, and remember, success usually lies in the detail.
- Ask how music, lighting, spatial arrangement etc. can play their part.
- Find appropriate texts to reinforce what should be happening.
- Choose the music.

Tip: use as few words as possible. Words restrict the effectiveness of symbolic action rather than enhance it.

As the world seems to be rediscovering the power of symbol the Bible offers us a treasury of new images that can enhance our worship and enable our formation. This might be especially useful for those who are suspicious of the traditional use of symbols because of their supposed Catholic overtones. Ironically, a more literal use of the Bible in worship might open doors to a new way of worshipping and to a power beyond imagining.

One step beyond this is the idea of enacting the liturgy.

Enacted liturgy

Imagine going to see *Hamlet*. You are sitting in your seat waiting for the performance to begin. The set looks magnificent. The impressive actors enter and begin but to your astonishment they hardly move. All they do is sit, stand and occasionally kneel. There is little, if any movement. The lighting never changes. It is a purely static presentation. Of course, this is an absurd scenario, but yet it is one that most of our congregations experience week after week as they see the greatest ever drama unfold.

A liturgical aeon ago, as an Anglican ordinand in the late 1970s, I spent a year in Rome, in a hitherto exclusively Roman Catholic school of spiritual formation run by the Focolare Movement. Daily I attended the community Mass but had to stay firmly in my seat while everyone else went for communion. To receive communion I had to travel the 15 miles into Rome each Sunday – quite a trek, though I used to liven it up with a secret trip to my favourite pizza bar.

For a short while an Anglican priest joined us. I made the most of this, insisting that he preside at the Eucharist every day he was there! While I revelled in this opportunity for spiritual gluttony, the one thing that remains in my memory is the *way* he celebrated the Eucharist – because it wasn't much of a celebration at all. He stood behind the altar in a surplice and stole with his hands hanging by his side. They never moved from start to finish except when he prepared the altar or turned a page. Something felt wrong. His spirit might have been celebrating the Eucharist but his body certainly wasn't. It was so dull. It proved to be a formative experience in my liturgical life, and the need to be creative in worship was firmly imprinted on my psyche.

To push the image further, we need to remember too that the congregation of worshippers is not the audience of the theatre but the main actors. All worship is a drama unfolding the greatest story we can ever hear, the story of the love of God. In worship we discover afresh God's love for us personally – at least, that is what is supposed to happen. Of course, worship is always *more* than drama, but drama it most certainly is. So if we want to present this drama more effectively perhaps we ought to take seriously the suggestion that we should dare to be a little more dramatic.

Posture and gesture

Some anthropologists, psychologists and philosophers might have the time to argue whether posture and gesture emanate from an internal attitude or create that inner attitude. Most people can find examples of both and there is certainly a clear relationship between the two. There are occasions when deep joy compels us to cry out – you only have to witness the behaviour at football stadiums week by week to see that. When your team scores, you jump up and down, wave your arms about, shout and maybe, if you are daring, you sing! That is an example of outward events creating an inner attitude that results in a change of posture and gesture. Many times I have visited the tomb of St Francis in Assisi, and on every occasion I was compelled to be silent and kneel. It is as if I have no choice. In both of those situations, there is a freedom to respond to the inner prompting in order to allow the inner attitude to be expressed physically. Sadly, in church such freedom is not usually given either explicitly or by virtue of the church culture through which we control the behaviour of worshippers. This not only dilutes our worship in the name of dignity, but actually undermines it.

Posture and gesture can also create an inner attitude. Take for example a prayer of confession. In my church we used to say the prayer of confession kneeling but with recent liturgical revision it has become the norm to 'confess' while standing. There are sound theological reasons why we should confess standing and I have no argument with them. We stand before God as forgiven sinners. I have preached it enough times to know that we are forgiven before we even ask, such is the awesomeness of what God has done in Jesus Christ. So we can *stand*. So much for the theology, but we must not let our theology become liturgical ideology. There are times when, like Isaiah, we particularly need to engage with our sinful nature and there is no doubt that kneeling to confess engenders a totally different attitude within us than that created by standing.

When we stand...	When we kneel...
our heads are up.	our heads are down.
we are in a position of acceptance.	we are in a position of begging for mercy.
we know our status.	we have no status.
we experience life and power.	we are humbled and weakened.

Each position engenders a different attitude, and our anaesthetised Church has really yet to come to terms with the idea of prostration, which is one step further down from kneeling.

So much for posture, but what about gesture? With the exception of charismatics,[1] the nearest most congregations come to using or changing gesture is when they put their service sheets or hymn books down. This is a pity because there are many possibilities:

- crossing our arms over our chest and bowing during confession;
- holding our palms up when we intercede;
- holding our arms out when we are praising;
- beating our chests in repentance;
- stretching our hands out towards someone if we are praying for them;
- making the sign of the cross.

The important question to ask is, 'What kind of attitude are we hoping to encourage in our worshippers, and what gesture will best encourage that?'

The use of (changes of) posture and gesture can be a powerful tool in our worship tool kit, so why do we not use it more often? One reason is dogmatism. There is a school of liturgy that tells us that there is a *right* and a *wrong* posture for each part of the service and they scoff when their rules are ignored. We need to move away from a rigorous, ideological approach to these issues towards one which displays a greater sensitivity to what a particular act of worship is trying to achieve. The key question is not 'Is it right according to the rubrics?' but 'Is it appropriate to the context, the theme and the flow?'

Space

The building we use for our worship is generally a 'given'. Unless we worship in a very adaptable environment most of us do not have the freedom to rearrange the 'set'. However, those who do have this possibility rarely seem to use the opportunities available to them, and those of us who complain about the settings we have inherited are often blinded by our complaints to what possibilities there might be. Most of the time we settle for a default arrangement without really exploring other possibilities.

I would encourage everyone to look at their 'set', preferably with someone else, and ask a simple question. What other way could it be arranged? The advantage of asking someone else, preferably someone who does not know your place of worship, is that they are more likely to see the possibilities than you are. I am not talking here about a radical reordering of our worship space, but simply a question of how we use the existing space available to us.

For example, where should the main leader of worship be positioned? No doubt there will be a customary place, and that is fine, but on some occasions it might be more appropriate for the leader to be somewhere else, perhaps even in the midst of the congregation. Where is the Bible read from? Is it read from a lectern at the front, or from the middle of the congregation signifying that the Bible is at the centre of the life of the Church? Where is the confession led from? From the front, by the leader, or from the font, signifying that forgiveness is part of the life of the baptised people of God?

Perhaps an extreme form of this is to explore the possibility of moving the congregation for different elements of the service. If the congregation is going to renew their baptismal promises, why not move towards the font? If the theme focuses on our unity as the Body of Christ, why not gather everyone around the holy table? Some churches now have one place to celebrate the liturgy of the Word and another to celebrate the liturgy of the sacrament. At the appropriate point everyone moves from one place to the other. The whole congregation then belongs to the offertory procession, and the people become the offering.

Some buildings lend themselves more to movement than others, but all of us have some flexibility if only we realise it. I suggest that 'Where?' should be a natural question to ask about each element of the service when we consider our planning.

Lighting

I recently visited a church that had seen through a beautiful £650,000 reordering of its worship space. It looked superb. I find sound desks irresistible, and what particularly drew me to this one was that I had been told it was a combined sound and lighting desk. I was shaking with excitement! When I approached, I could not believe my eyes. True, it was a combined sound and lighting desk, but the lighting element consisted of a set of straightforward on–off light switches. They had spent £650,000 but they had not included dimmer switches that would have given them a vast array of lighting possibilities, costing perhaps an extra £1,000. This betrays an attitude in churches that our lights are either on or off, and fails to see that lighting can be one of the most useful tools in the creation of an environment for worship.

The 'Ahh moments' I described earlier happen when we are moved by the environment and the worship, when everything seems to work together to give us a profound sense of God. I would wager that for the overwhelming majority of us, these are occasions when the church lighting is at the very least subdued, and probably off altogether.

On a youth weekend with a group of fairly lively, if not rebellious, kids, it became increasingly clear that even a short service in the large lounge was going to be risky. The leaders' anxiety mounted at the thought of trying to sing hymns, pray, preach a sermon, and all the things that you do in normal services. We could imagine the sniggers of the kids evolving into giggles; the quick tickle from one developing into a fight; the rude noises increasing in volume as we tried to unfold to them the mysteries of Jesus the Light of the World. We decided that the only course open to us was to do something totally different.

We trekked from the centre about half a mile to a small cave. Each person was given a candle and we went in. We climbed over rocks and went around a couple of bends, until we reached a point where we could all stand together. There, in the pitch black, it became easy to talk about Jesus the Light of the World. We sang hymns, blew out our candles and prayed about the darkness in our own lives and in the world. Most of the kids prayed aloud in the absolute darkness. Then, one by one we lit the candles and just watched the impact. Jesus the Light of the World really did not need to be preached because they had experienced him. The kids were stunned by the power of the worship and were almost silent as we started back.

If the use of light and darkness can be so powerful, why do we not use it more in worship? Why not sometimes switch (some of) the lights out for the confession and switch them on again when the minister pronounces the absolution? Why not use the lights we have to highlight different areas of the church as is appropriate for the service? Why not spotlight different people or objects at different times? None of this demands a clever lighting system in the church. It just involves using the lighting we have, or maybe moving the occasional spotlight, but if you have a spare £500 or so I would suggest that the most useful way it could be spent would be to replace your church's on–off switches with dimmers.

One Holy Week was made to feel different simply by adjusting the lighting. Rather than use the main church lights we used two overhead projectors placed at the back of the church. On Maundy Thursday we covered the OHP in a blue transparency, on Good Friday we used red, and on Easter Day we used yellowy gold. The light made an amazing difference to the church, and to the people's experience, all done with the most basic equipment.

The secular world learned a long time ago that you can do extraordinary things with light and darkness. They can alter mood; they can create silence; they can give a sense of security; they can liberate; they can uplift. Why is the Church so slow to learn these very simple truths, and then use them?

Decoration

Most of us are used to decoration in church, and the impact such a change of decoration can make. Churches are centres for floral excellence. Sometimes they are better known in the community for their flower arrangements than their praying. We are also well versed on the way the atmosphere of a church changes when we remove flowers in Lent and maybe Advent. Suddenly the building looks austere, bare, challenging.

We are used to this, but what about the rest of the year? And what about other kinds of decoration even during these two bare seasons? Most of the time, like lighting, we have either all or nothing. But why should it be like this? There is nothing to stop the decoration of the church fitting the liturgical theme. If it is a celebratory theme, why not decorate the church appropriately? If the theme is the cross, or sacrifice, or martyrdom, why not make red the predominant colour of the arrangements? Or maybe even think beyond the flowers and use red drapes, or use a hint of red in the lighting?

It is the tradition in many churches after the Maundy Thursday Eucharist to remove all hangings and decoration from the worship area in preparation for Good Friday. At the end of the Eucharist of the Last Supper the ministers go around the church, and slowly everything is removed item by item. I have always approached this with more than just a little self-consciousness. But on one such occasion I found a new member of our church in tears in her pew. She had just joined us from an independent charismatic church so my first reaction was, 'Did it look *that* silly?' But as I talked to her I realised how deeply moved she had been as the church had been stripped. 'Look what they have done to Jesus!' was all she could really say. The removal of all the ordinary decorative items had made a profound impact on her, just as it is supposed to do. If our surroundings can have such an impact on us on these special occasions, why not apply the same principles to what we do week by week?

Transitions

Someone has made the comment that when the cinema audience watch a film they go ready to enter into the world that is presented to them. There is an innate willingness to share in the fictional 'reality' of the film and to suspend their participation in the everyday world. However, when people go to church they take with them the joys and pains of the world and are usually less willing to enter into the world of worship.

One of the reasons for this is that when you go into a cinema (or a theatre) a lot of thought has been given to how to prepare you to watch the film or play. The entrance to modern cinemas is designed to give the impression that you are entering another world. You are ushered down carpeted corridors with images of the films on show around you. There is a subliminal sense of heightened excitement. You enter a dark auditorium that hushes you. You find a comfortable seat and slide down into it. Then lights go up and down, and curtains open and close as the advertisements come on. And so it goes on. The watching public is made ready for the main event, by which time they are more than willing to enter into the world of Middle Earth or whatever it might be.

How different it is when we go to church!

The way in which we are prepared before the service actually begins is of profound significance for the way we relate to what follows. For example some friends prepared themselves to see *Hamlet* by reading it together over breakfast for several weeks before the performance. If only Christians showed that kind of committed preparation for worship! Like those friends of ours, worshippers have to take some responsibility for the way they come to church. We could be encouraged to study the readings and to do some self-examination at home before we start our journey. The church might even suggest some prayers for the journey to church to distance people from the over-soapy water of the rushed breakfast washing-up!

But what happens when we arrive? How do we make the transition from the world of washing-up to the world of worship? The same applies equally to the dismissal rites of the Church. How is the congregation enabled to go back into the world and to make appropriate connections with what has happened in worship? Indeed, how can our transitional rites help make this whole journey one of experience and faith, encouraging us into a sense of expectation that we will have a life-changing encounter with the living God which we will carry with us into the next week?

Music

At school I hated cross-country running. I intensely disliked having to wade through icy puddles and have mud clinging to my bare legs. But when the weekly choice between music and cross-country was presented to us there was no contest. The damp air of the woods around the school always won. Consequently I am not a musician. I just about know how many beats there are to a minim and when the notes go up or down, but by how much I just have to guess. Anything beyond that takes me into the realms of a mystery I prefer not to explore. But just as you do not need to be a quantum physicist to appreciate the power of nuclear weapons, so you do not need to know the finer points of music theory to appreciate its power, especially in worship.

It has been suggested that the hymn 'When I survey the wondrous cross' is an example of a tune perfectly matching the words. How that kind of measurement can really be made is open to question, but the commentators certainly had a point. For three hundred years it has led people to gaze in wonder and awe at the cross of Christ, and has become a vehicle for expressing our most profound thanksgiving for the love shown to us through the death of Jesus. It has moved hearts of every age, every race and every time by its wonderful poetry and music, which form an unparalleled combination.

Imagine the effect if we were only allowed to say the words rather than sing them – or we had to listen to the tune instead of singing along. The impact would be more than halved.[2] When music is used to enhance the beautiful poetry of the words the resulting effect is far more than the sum of the parts. Music has the potential to do this with almost every aspect of worship. It can take words, lift them from the purely cerebral and transform them until those same words minister to our hearts.

The world has been aware of this for some time. In the classic 1949 RKO film *Mighty Joe Young*, the playing of 'Beautiful Dreamer'[3] pacified the gorilla, and the audience did not find it surprising that music could be used to pacify even this great beast. Since then the secular and scientific world has continued to become ever more aware of the power of music. Music at airports calms the crowds as they prepare to fly. Music is used in exactly the opposite way at ice hockey matches, to wind up the crowd and keep them in a constant state of excitement. Before a theatre or cinema show the music piped to the audience is specifically designed to engender the right mood in the waiting public. Music is played to unborn children because it is thought to stimulate their brain cells, and music therapy is a now well-established part of medicine. Music has the ability to touch the deepest elements of our humanity bringing not just calm but healing.

Yet once again the world has left the Church on the starting blocks when it comes to using these wonderful gifts of creation. Music in church has primarily limited itself to the predictable organ voluntaries or hymns. It is used to break up the long sequences of words or to provide a pleasing distraction while some movement or action has to be performed.

In theory the hymns break up the service into easily consumable pieces. In reality they hold the whole thing together because the congregation tend to prefer the musical items to any of the others – the hymns are the bits most people look forward to. In the space between arriving and the beginning of the service many will check to see what hymns are being sung, but I have never seen people looking with eagerness to see what eucharistic prayer will be used. I have never heard shouts of acclamation along the lines of 'Yes! We are going to use the prayer of humble access!' I have, however, heard that said, or rather shouted, about some songs and hymns.

Our expectations about what music can do, and our willingness to exploit it, are far behind the secular world. In 1992 a symposium was held in Milwaukee[4] to look at the role of music in worship. The result was a document that opened up new horizons for church musicians. They made a distinction between what was called 'Music at the Ritual' and 'Ritual Music'. 'Music at the Ritual' comprises those hymns and organ voluntaries that function like commas or full stops in the liturgy: for example a hymn between readings from the Bible; the organ voluntaries at the beginning and end, or while an offering is being taken; the solo while people receive communion. 'Ritual Music', however, is music which forms an integral part (of the liturgy), weaving itself into the whole structure and fabric of the worship. It is more than just singing parts of the Eucharist rather than saying them; it is where the music has been specifically chosen to enable a smooth flow through the liturgy. It is not about deciding where to put a hymn, but about exploring ways in which music can be used as a tool to enable each element of the worship to fulfil its proper task.

Truly effective church musicians need to know far more than how to play hymns well, or to lead congregational singing. Music provides a powerful tool for enabling worship to move smoothly from one mood to another. If the leader wants to move a congregation from an exuberant hymn of praise into a period of reflection before the confession, words of direction may have some effect, but music will enable this to happen far more effectively and will bring an added dimension to the liturgy. Music is a language that seems to make the heart more open to God.

The reverse is also the case. Music can be a vehicle through which God opens his heart to us. Some are beginning to journey into the new territory of music and intercession. Many churches are now familiar with the 'voice-over' prayer where the leader speaks while a musician plays, but this is really only the tip of the iceberg of possibilities. The replacement of the spoken word by music and images in intercession takes us into a previously unexplored landscape. Images may be used, or short sentences projected onto a wall or screen while instrumentalists offer an improvised response. In this way the musicians, 'playing in the Spirit', can communicate the heart of God for his world.[5]

A Brazilian pastor sought prayer at a large gathering. All that the congregation could see was one person praying with him as he knelt. An oboist approached them and began to play a haunting lament. He finished, then moved off. I later learned that the Brazilian pastor had asked for prayer because he had recently lost his young son, and while I have no doubt that the prayer of the priest praying with that man was effective and was a vehicle for healing his deep pains, somehow I suspect that the channel of grace was opened much more by the spontaneous oboe lament. The man concerned certainly felt the added dimension of spoken and musical prayer.

This effect could not have been accomplished if the musician concerned had only been able to play set pieces. He had to be accomplished enough, and bold enough, to break away from the set music and 'play in the Spirit'. That may be some way from where most of our church musicians are, but it is something to aim for.

Many churches are hamstrung because the musicians determine what happens in services. This is not their role or their gift. Let the gifted worship planners, not the musicians, be the ones to set the flow of the worship, but involve the musicians fully in the planning of *how* to make that flow work. All churches can break out of voluntary/hymn/anthem mode by working more closely with the musicians and asking appropriate questions. How can music help us to make each transition through the different elements of worship? How can a particular prayer be made more effective by music gently playing underneath the words? How can silence be aided by a musical introduction and possibly a musical conclusion?

Manipulation

The word *manipulation* has only taken on a pejorative meaning over the past few decades with the rise of various cult practices that force people to act against their natural inclination. But the original meaning of the word means 'to handle well'. We manipulate objects into their true position. It does not mean 'to bypass a person's freedom'. Manipulation can be used for good or for bad and some of the services of the early Church, particularly the initiation rites, show evidence of far more manipulative behaviour than we would dare to engage in today.

Some might also say that this use of music, and by implication lighting, drama, colour, special effects, etc., is no more than emotionalism and a more subtle form of manipulation where we create the most conducive environment for a particular response, but this is something our media society does all the time. Advertisers use all those tools to encourage you to buy their product, but we do not accuse them of manipulation. The lover does their best to create the perfect environment to 'pop the question'. We never object when people act after hearing a compelling argument. But who is to say that the presentation of an argument is no more than manipulation of our rational faculties? The use of music simply appeals to the non-rational and intuitive faculties. Reacting to them is neither better nor worse than reacting after hearing a well-presented argument. Music used well does not force us to go where we do not want to venture, but enables us more easily to flow with the Spirit of God.

The power that music can have over people has tended to make worship leaders wary of using it to its fullest potential. If creativity is about creating the total environment for liturgy to do its job of leading us to a formative encounter with God surely we ought to do everything within our power and use all reasonable means to make that happen? Yet we need to treat these resources with care. Music is a powerful implement in the liturgist's tool kit. It can transform our worship from pedestrian to exhilarating, but we need to ensure that it is used to draw out the essential meaning of the worship rather than add something unnecessary to it, which not only confuses the message but also dilutes its power.

Dirty Harry's dictum – A man's got to know his limitations

Even before planning it is useful to ask what things you control and what you do not. Our worship is affected and effected by a whole bagful of influences, some of which we have control over and some of which we do not. Some of these elements might be:

- the architecture of the building
- the order of service – i.e. the text and rubrics we use

- music
- lighting
- posture and gesture
- furniture
- weather
- the morale of the congregation
- the sum of personal circumstances of the people
- the social context (locally, nationally and even worldwide).[6]

When we prepare for worship these and other factors will affect what we do, how we do it, and how it is understood. Sometimes it might be helpful to be aware of the things we can control and those we cannot. For example, we have no control over the architecture of the building (though there may be a long-term impact if a reordering scheme is considered), the weather, the morale of the people (though this could be changed in the short or medium term), the sum of the personal circumstances of the congregation and the social context. However, most of us do have some control over the order of service, the music, the posture and gesture to be adopted and the way the furniture is arranged. It is counter-productive if we try to build an act of worship around things that cannot be changed. This will usually lead to frustration on the part of both the leaders and congregation. However, there are often far more dimensions that can be used than we realise.

Over-indulgence

I love Christmas lunch. I love the over-indulgence of rich food. I am usually salivating over the prospect of turkey with two kinds of stuffing accompanied by sausage and mushroom and bacon; the sweetcorn cooked with almonds in butter, and Brussels sprouts drenched in garlic butter. All this is followed by British Christmas pudding so rich with dried fruit that it falls apart when you light the brandy on it and pour lashings of fresh, thick double cream onto it. I can already feel the need to loosen the belt on my trousers. But I could not eat it every day, at least not without going to the gym far, far more often than I do.

The same is true of worship. Formative worship offers us a

balanced diet that will build us up into fit Christians, not spiritually flabby disciples. Liturgy, like good food, needs a balance
between light and substantial, rich and refreshing. Too much
rich food is indigestible. If you tried to produce a service where
every element had gone through a rigorous questioning, you
would end up with such a rich diet that would do no good for
any church. Not only would it be too rich for a congregation to
digest, but the service would take up most of Sunday. Ideally,
asking the kinds of questions I have raised throughout this book
would be part of the process. Over a period of time questions
could be asked of every part, each question explored at an appropriate time, and each answer implemented as and when
appropriate.

The most effective way to allow the kind of worship I am
suggesting is to be selective in what you do and limited in what
you aim for week by week. Do not try to make the whole of the
service one long encounter with God for everyone: it will give
them spiritual indigestion.

Summary

*In this chapter I have tried to suggest ways in which we can
develop our worship so that it becomes an environment where
individuals within the congregation might have a formative
encounter with God. The leader's task is not to put power in, but
to draw it out. To do this effectively and sensitively we need to
use all those means at our disposal: music, word, light, silence,
imagination, setting, symbol, etc. The difficult task is to use these
means to draw out the power of worship rather than to obscure
it. I hope I have offered questions that might be asked and an
approach that might be employed so that we use every available
means to draw people into that meeting place with the divine.*

Conclusion
Freeing Worship

It is a sunny day at the end of June. The sound of bells floats over the cathedral city rooftops announcing that a new army of clergy will be tackling and solving the problems of the Church and the world.

They have reason to be hopeful. They have in their hands God's tools for transforming the individual, the Church and the whole of creation, but will they recognise them, and use them to their full potential? Or will they use them in the one-dimensional way with which the Church has become accustomed, and which tends to anaesthetise the world rather than transform it?

In this book I have tried to do a number of things:

- raise the vision of what worship could be;
- give some practical suggestions about how this might be achieved;
- offer some ways to understand what might be happening in worship; and
- encourage us to move from the safety of our current pasture to greener grass.

If worship is the environment where we become what God calls us to be, then we are not simply dealing with words, music, space, lighting, symbol and action. The raw material of true worship is our humanity in all its glory and all its shame. When worship works it will evoke within us deep reactions of joy or antagonism because it will be challenging the boundaries of our comfort zone and opening new possibilities of what we might be. This is not always a pleasant experience.

As a parish priest I am aware of the huge gap between what is and what could be. The week-by-week experience of many obscures the visionary calling. Those who try to walk towards the future that calls them, and dare to take those first few steps towards that alluring voice, often hear a hundred more urging them in the opposite directions towards a non-existent, glorious past.

At the heart of this is a pastoral tension which we face in every sphere of church life, but I want to encourage worship leaders to hear God's call to 'Come!' rather than the myriad voices that scream 'Stay!' The American preacher John Wimber used to say that the word *faith* is actually spelt R-I-S-K. Growth without risk is no more than a mirage that draws us towards an almost certain death in a waterless desert. Standing still is not an option unless we are happy to fade into the shadows of irrelevance. The real shepherd will encourage the sheep from the comfortable fields of the present, that will surely run out of sustenance, towards the greener, grass-filled fields of the future.

Does it work?

While on sabbatical I had lunch with Cindy. She was a final-year student in theology at the University of Notre Dame in Indiana and had been given the resources to take me to lunch, always a good way to get my attention. Cindy felt called to teach the faith and she was concerned about spiritual growth. Her desire was to see Christians growing in their relationship with God, each other and the whole of creation. Gently she raised a subject that makes liturgists turn red-faced with embarrassment. She pointed out that for decades, liturgists have claimed that worship 'forms' the people of God. In her experience this is no more than liturgical idealism. 'Where,' she asked, 'is the evidence that this is happening? Does worship really "form" the people of God?'

This is a difficult question for liturgists. Too often we can appear like high-minded architects who design a fantastic construction. In our enthusiasm for its eye-catching beauty we fail to ask the key question – will it work?[1]

Making worship work has been a particular interest of mine but I had to concede to Cindy that there is limited evidence of this in the mainstream Churches, though no doubt somewhere one church must be getting it right. There are examples of spiritual formation going hand in hand with worship, but usually in a community context, such as at Taizé in France, or Iona in Scotland. I believe that the answer to Cindy's question is 'Yes'. I may be naïve, but I am convinced that worship really can form the people of God and even transform creation.

Can you share that same vision? Could you be encouraged to take the necessary risks to turn that vision into reality?

Notes

Chapter 1   Word, Word, Word!

1. For a more detailed history of the philosophy and culture of this period see *Reformation Thought* by Alister E. McGrath, published by Blackwell 1999.
2. It is also an interesting irony that just as the printing press enabled the imposition of a liturgical dictatorship by enabling texts to be freely and cheaply produced it was the Internet, the twentieth century's equivalent invention, which finally put the nail in the coffin of that same uniformity.
3. Rubrics are instructions for the way a service or ceremony is to be conducted.
4. *Roman Catholic Worship: Trent to Today* by James F. White, published by Paulist Press, New York, 1995.
5. 'Ritual, change, and changing ritual' by Catherine Bell in *Worship* 63 (1989), pp. 31–41.
6. Figures quoted from *The Reformation* by Owen Chadwick, published by Pelican 1964.
7. As James White has argued in his *Introduction to Worship*, published by Nashville Press, Abingdon, 1991, especially in the chapter on the Enlightenment.
8. Of course this is a rational mistake. Really all he could conclude is that 'I think, therefore there is thinking'. In fact the 'I' itself could be a delusion, but why spoil a good party?
9. Mark Searle of the University of Notre Dame, Indiana, suggests these first three. I added the others.
10. Actually the Verification Principle does not hold true. Philosophers such as Karl Popper showed that the scientific method is based on a Negation Principle not a Verification Principle. Ian Ramsey and Karl Popper effectively attacked Ayer. However, the importance of logical positivism lies not in its truth or falsity but in the way it has become part of popular philosophy and culture in the twentieth century.
11. It is interesting that one of the other major philosophical movements of the twentieth century, linguistic analysis initiated by Ludwig Wittgenstein, in his book *Tractatus Logico-Philosophicus*, published by Routledge and Kegan Paul 1961, should focus on the limits of language and its meaning. This fascination continued throughout Wittgenstein's

life and illustrates the domination of the word/mind axis in our time and why it continues to dominate the thinking of the producers of liturgy today.

Chapter 2   Worship in Four Dimensions

1. *The Westminster Shorter Catechism*, Question 1.

Chapter 3   *Transforming Worship*

1. *Reflections on the Psalms* by C. S. Lewis, now available in *The Inspirational Writings of C S Lewis*, published by Budget Books Service Inc. 1994.
2. At time of writing Cyril Ashton is the Anglican Bishop of Doncaster in England.
3. From Rt Revd Cyril Ashton's MA thesis for Lancaster University 1986.
4. Quoted in Arnold Bittlinger, *Gifts and Graces*, published by Eerdmans, Grand Rapids 1967.
5. Douglas Davies, 'Social groups, liturgy, and glossolalia' in *The Churchman*, vol. 90, no. 3, London 1977.
6. *Class, Codes and Control*, vols 1–3, published by Routledge and Kegan Paul in 1971, 1973 and 1975.
7. Translation from *Common Worship*, published by Church House Publishing, London, 2000.
8. This is from the deuterocanonical section of the Book of Daniel.

Chapter 4   Living Worship

1. *Lent – Holy Week – Easter*, published jointly by Church House Publishing, Cambridge University Press and SPCK, 1984, 1986.
2. His phrase, not mine.
3. Published by Bright Mountain Books, North Carolina, 1992.
4. *Baptism and Eucharist: Ecumenical Convergence in Celebration*, edited by Max Thurian and Geoffrey Wainwright, published by the World Council of Churches, Geneva, as a follow-up to the WCC 'Lima text' of *Baptism, Eucharist and Ministry*. Although texts of both baptism and eucharistic services have been revised considerably since then the convergence in those documents had added to the thesis of this book.
5. Ronald Grimes is Professor of Religion and Culture at Wilfrid Laurier University in Waterloo, Ontario, Canada. He wrote an influential article called 'Liturgical supinity, liturgical erectitude: on the embodiment of ritual authority', published in *Worship* (1993), pp. 51–69.
6. Ibid., p.52.

Chapter 5 Parabolic Worship

1. From *Art and Psychology* by W. H. Auden, pp. 18–19, quoted in the article 'Tell it slant' by John Tinsley in *Theology*, vol. 83 (May/June 1980), published by SPCK, London.
2. *Living Stories of the Cherokee*, collected and edited by Barbara R. Duncan, published by the University of North Carolina Press, Asheville, 1998.
3. Told by Freeman Owle and quoted by Barbara Duncan in *Living Stories of the Cherokee*, pp. 226–8.
4. 'Tell it slant' by John Tinsley.

Chapter 6 Symbolic Worship

1. The meaning of the words 'introverted' and 'extroverted' are taken from the Myers Briggs Personality Type Indicator.
2. See Michael Marshall's Book, *Free to Worship*, published by Marshall Pickering 1996, where he writes about the curse of the tidy sacristan.

Chapter 7 Engaging Worship

1. The gift of tongues is often misunderstood and is manifested in a number of different forms. There is the public speaking out in a tongue by one person where an interpretation should follow. There is the personal use of the gift for and within private prayer, and there is the corporate use of tongues in the context of singing in the Spirit. It is these latter two that I am concerned with here.
2. *Common Worship: Pastoral Service*, published by Church House Publishing 2001, p. 105.
3. I am aware that in some traditions once the Easter candle is lit, it remains lit, but the act of lighting a candle powerfully represents the resurrection.

Chapter 8 Creating Worship

1. Even here the use of different gestures in charismatic worship tends to be limited to arm movement or flag-waving. I have noticed that in different charismatic contexts different gestures are used, but most members of such congregations do tend to behave in ways that are considered acceptable to that particular body. While I have often seen people moved to dance, which I consider laudable, rarely have I seen anyone moved to prostrate themselves. The charismatic context usually offers more freedom, but even that freedom is limited by what is and is not locally observable and socially acceptable.
2. Singing it to another tune can also have an impact as it encourages people to focus on the words as they try to fit them to a new tune.

3. Written by Stephen Collins Foster.
4. *The Milwaukee Symposia for Church Composers*: a ten-year report by the Washington, DC National Association of Pastoral Musicians, published by Liturgy Training Publications, Chicago IL, 1992. See also *Music and Liturgy: The Universa Laus Document and Commentary* by Claude Duscheneau and Michel Veuthey, translated by Paul Inwood, published by Pastoral Press, Washington, DC, 1992.
5. This kind of intercessory music has been pioneered in Britain by Wellspring. See www.wellspring.org.uk
6. A service celebrated on 10 September 2001 would have been very different from exactly the same service celebrated on 12 September 2001 after the World Trade Center towers had fallen following the terrorist attack.

Conclusion   Freeing Worship

1. Like the wonderful, but flawed, Millennium Bridge in London.